D1466512

Crucial Problems
of Modern Philosophy

by

D. J. B. HAWKINS

With an Introduction

by

JOHN P. DOLAN

UNIVERSITY OF NOTRE DAME PRESS
1962

Introduction

The deep sense of a need for reappraisal that has transcended all of the disciplines in recent decades is perhaps nowhere more in evidence than in the perplexities that confront the serious student of philosophy. It is becoming more and more apparent that philosophical problems, like historical concepts, stand in need of re-examination. Like coins that pass from hand to hand unnoticed, they often bear, in the light of closer scrutiny, a stamp that is not as sharp and clear as one would assume. In this provocative little work Dr. Hawkins proposes "a discussion sticking more closely to history" as a means for illucidating the more common-sense elements of present-day philosophy.

Any intellectual system that attempts to operate outside the framework of history loses much of its formative power. It has taken two centuries to recover from the rationalistic attack on the theological interpretation of history, and there are few indications that the hypnotic trance that often stratifies and stagnates in the over-generous filing system of what is mistakenly called Thomism is losing its grip today. We must convince ourselves that there can be no *philosophia perennis* without a *traditio historica*. The perennial element of any ideology connotes the very notion of history as an uninterrupted welling up of life in a multitude of divisions, currents, and countercurrents formed by changing influences and varied impulses. Yet quite recently a well-known spokesman of Neo-Thomism has asserted that he "was not interested in any new turn towards religion among intellectuals. Nor even in any new turn or new historic orientation towards religion." Historical absolutism, the reluctance to relinquish non-dogmatic doctrines, often overlooks the all-important fact that the basic function of philosophy is to bring into play the total body of truth known to man. Philosophy like theology must integrate the divine message as it encounters man in the shape of the historical image, symbol, or event as well as the structure of particular culture. Humanity really understands the new only when it inherits much of the old. Filiation is a pervading aspect of the philosophical quest, and Scholasticism, like Western culture itself, did not grow autochthonously from its own soil. Cross-relations between schools of philosophy have invariably produced stronger hybrids. It is one of the paradoxes of history that the Catholic Cardinal Cusa, who heralded the modern era in philosophy by giving a new dimension to the perennial problem of reconciling God and man, and whose cosmology so well suited the widening horizons of the visible world, enscribed as disciples none of those whose rightful heritage was the *philosophia perennis*. An open-minded approach to his scientific philosophy might well have avoided the repeated and embarrassing blunders that have plagued the body politic of the Church from Galileo to Mivart. Philosophy has remained in many areas what Brownson called it a century ago—"some fragment of Catholic theology badly proved."

Revisionism and reversalism are the very substrata of all Western thought from idealism to materialism, from transcendentalism to immanentism. The concepts remain the same irrespective of the systems in which they operate. If the systems are inadequate, at least the

6

problems they pose are relevant. The reversals of late antiquity had their counterpart in the disintegration of Scholasticism. They have their parallels today. The analytical spirit of Descartes may have dominated all fields of thought after the middle of the seventeenth century. Yet it was seriously challenged by the philosophy of Leibnitz, thus giving a new direction to all Western philosophy. The *scientia generalis* of the latter, the alphabet of ideas that he envisioned, was not far in purpose and scope from the *summae* of the medieval world. Both operated on the premise that there is no solution to the problem of truth independently of the problem of God, since knowledge of the divine being forms the highest principle of knowledge from which all other evaluations are deduced. If the *summae* are outmoded, there is some consolation in the fact that the historic Thomas can be found in the *Quaestiones disputatae,* where the end-product is a mutual exploration of problems aimed not so much at overcoming an opponent as towards opening a new vista of truth. The *recherche collective de la vérité* of the Middle Ages placed no limits on the subject considered and spared no one in the quest for ultimates. Man's quest for truth like his quest for God must be brought to bear on the whole of natural knowledge of the world and existence. There is a growing awareness, even among Thomists, that Scholasticism was at most a compromise that achieved a delicate balance under the brilliant influence of Aquinas. Yet it was a balance that was upset by the very same intellectual forces it attempted to reconcile. There is an increasing conviction that a failure to bring into play the total body of truths known to man will inevitably upset even the most closely integrated system. The growing boundaries of natural knowledge place the well-ordered categories of the scholastic synthesis beyond the hope of philosopher, scientist, or theologian to reach a premature unity. The cult of rationalizing on the periphery of cultural, economic, or political facts is a luxury that the age can no longer afford. For too many, Divus Thomas has been transformed to a position where one no longer evaluates but adores. Thomas has vanished behind his work. Msgr. Raemymaeker of the Thomistic Institute of Louvain, in discussing the failure of so many Thomists to teach Thomistic philosophy, has insisted that these teachers are not Thomists, and that the essence of the philosophy of St. Thomas Aquinas is the living application of principles to the thought and problems of the day.

The Kantian desire to reduce conscience to a formalistic dictate independent of emotion and authority was motivated by a deep and perduring pietism. His impact on the intellectual world is a challenge that cannot be dismissed with a few classroom clichés. In giving rise to a new anthropology, it raised questions revolving about man's personality and cultural environment that awoke moralists to the danger of utilitarianism and provided ossified casuistry with a stimulating challenge. The anticipatory element injected into Western thought by Hegel cannot be ignored any more than the reversal of Hegel by Marx. The Marxist dialectic has a messianic element that is deep in Christian tradition. It resembles in many respects the faith in Providence that characterized the medieval period and that directs all human struggle towards a final harmony. His analysis of bourgeois society bears closely on the eschatological hope that was so much a part of early Christianity. It helped to awaken the Church from the long slumber into which indifference to social problems had lulled it. Challenging too is the existentialist philosophy of Kierkegaard. His measuring of the so-called Christianity lived by Christians against the real Christianity produces a confrontation that is startling. His call to a realization of vitalized faith as an existential striving for existence is a transition from a possibility in spirit to a reality in the wholeness of the person. His concern for the most fundamental problem that faces the perennial philosophy, the problem of communication, cannot be overlooked. That these efforts in the past were beset with failures should not mean that they be ignored today any more than identity of purpose should imply mere repetition or imitation.

Readers will find in this penetrating work a common-sense appraisal of the role of philosophy in today's crucial problems. They will see in it the underlying conviction that the best achievement of human thought may be considered as the extension of the Incarnation, as the product of a grace which is gradually composing the climate necessary for its flowering.

JOHN P. DOLAN

Contents

CRUCIAL PROBLEMS
OF MODERN PHILOSOPHY

Foreword

THE student of philosophy is today in a difficult position. It is only healthy-minded to hope to reach a philosophy which yields some genuine and positive insight into the nature of things. For examples of such philosophizing we rightly look back to the Greeks, especially to Plato and to Aristotle, and increased knowledge of the Middle Ages enables us more and more clearly to see the syntheses of the thirteenth century as heirs of the Hellenic tradition. If later philosophy had continued to develop on these lines, the contemporary thinker would be presented with a fair prospect of attaining his positive goal.

But philosophy has not developed in a straight line. A study of thought since the Middle Ages faces us with an immense complexity of new questions which, whether the answers be left in doubt or they be answered in any of the various ways suggested by the most prominent of modern philosophers, seem to bar the possibility of reaching a satisfactory positive philosophy. The hopes entertained by philosophers of the results of their inquiries have become progressively more modest.

If the contemporary student could rightfully dismiss modern philosophy as a collection of pernickety attempts to question the unquestionable, he could go ahead gaily enough. But it is only too clear that the questions asked have been legitimate and even inevitable. We might seem at present to be faced with the dilemma of either taking refuge from difficulties in a gratuitous dogmatism or relapsing into some form of fashionable triviality.

The memory of my own difficulties and hesitations prevents me from underrating the force with which this dilemma appears to many minds. I do not see how any candid-minded person at present can reach a positive philosophy without passing through such a period of perplexity. But since I think that we should be able to pass through it and to attain a metaphysic in continuity with the Greek and medieval tradition, I want here to try to throw into relief what seem to be the main causes of perplexity and the main obstacles to a more positive kind of philosophizing than is now usually cultivated. And, when the difficulties are isolated, I want the reader to ask himself whether they are really as great as they first appear and are generally supposed to be.

Above all, there are the questions of the scope of experience and of the power of thought. Is human experience really as restricted as the philosophers who are called empiricists thought it to be? Are what Kant called synthetic *a priori* propositions or, as they might be called, non-tautological entailments, really to be ruled out as immediate insights into the nature of things? I have already outlined what I hold to be given as facts of experience in *The Criticism of Experience* (1945) and the general metaphysic which can be built upon them in *Being and Becoming* (1954), but it may be that a discussion sticking more closely to history, such as is here attempted, will be of interest to some readers.

The chapter on "Wittgenstein and the Cult of Language" has recently appeared as an Aquinas Paper (Blackfriars Publications). Three other chapters are reprinted from periodicals, "The Philosophical Background of Marx and Engels" from *Blackfriars* (Feb. 1953), "Philosophy and Common Sense" from *Colosseum* (Dec. 1936), and "The Enlargement of Empiricism" from *The Wind and the Rain* (Autumn 1948). I am grateful to Fr. Illtud Evans, O.P., Mr. Bernard Wall and Mr. Neville Braybrooke respectively for their willingness that these articles should be reproduced.

D.J.B.H.

Part I

THE PRECURSORS

CHAPTER I

Descartes and the Project of a Critical Theory of Knowledge

I

WHATEVER else may be said for or against Descartes, it is evident that he gave philosophy a new direction which has continued down to the present day. The project of a systematic theory of knowledge is his. He asked what were the primary and unassailable data of experience and what else was susceptible of full critical justification by following from such data. Philosophers have gone on asking these questions ever since.

Only recently has the suggestion gained ground that the Cartesian quest is vain. Can we go beyond the data of experience? Perhaps, as the logical positivists hold, we can only talk about them in different ways. More radically, are there any primary and unassailable data? If not, the whole Cartesian approach is vitiated, and we must look for a new direction in philosophy.

New approaches in philosophy are certainly not to be condemned as such. Half the fun of philosophy, to put the matter in its lowest terms, arises from the different points of view from which different philosophers approach their subject. We may still, however, legitimately ask whether the Cartesian quest is outdated. If we do, we are now compelled to ask not simply what are the primary data of experience, but what, if any, are the primary data of experience, and not simply how do we get beyond them but how, if at all, we get beyond them.

The contention here will be that the Cartesian programme has not outlasted its usefulness. Only an unduly restricted conception of the data of experience has made philosophers despair of establishing such data at all, and only a view of the powers of thought which confines its achievements to tautologies or hypotheses has made them despair of a constructive metaphysic. Historically, we have then to ask whether the empiricists were really faithful to experience and what is the real import of the kind of proposition which Kant described as synthetic *a priori*.

Hence we begin with comments on Descartes, on the classical empiricists and on Kant. We go on to discuss how contemporary philosophers attack or retreat from our problems, and conclude with four chapters of a more positive kind. The last of these concerns the possibility, for a thinker of today, of returning with a clear conscience to the tradition of Aristotle and the medieval scholastics, for this possibility is evidently dependent on coping satisfactorily with the epistemological problems of modern times.

II

In the first flush of the medieval revival Descartes was sometimes regarded as a regrettable incident in the history of philosophy, the beginning of a rot which was similarly held to have grown progressively worse as time went on. From a less exclusive and more adequate point of view the Cartesian project appears as a necessary completion of the systematization of knowledge which Aristotle adumbrated in the *Posterior Analytics*. There Aristotle aims at exhibiting human knowledge as a harmonious development from evident first principles.

Looking back from our distance in time we perceive one chief error and one chief omission in the scheme of the *Posterior Analytics*. The error was the assumption that this direct axiomatic method could be applied to the subject-matter of the physical sciences. The corporeal world is not as intrinsically intelligible as Aristotle supposed it to be, and it is the merit of seventeenth-century science from Galileo onwards to have begun to apply with full effect those less direct but more fruitful methods of investigation with which we are now familiar.

It was also in the seventeenth century that the attempt was made to repair the omission. For Aristotle's maxims were derived from completely abstract fields of knowledge, such as logic and metaphysics and (in spite of his apparent distaste for mathematics) mathematics also; and it did not occur to him that a parallel systematization was needed in respect of the material of our knowledge, the sorts of things that we are able to know. This omission, by asking what precisely were objects of experience and what precisely could be inferred from experience, Descartes sought to remedy. We must therefore say that his project, whatever he may have thought of it himself and however others have sometimes judged it, was an expansion and completion of the Aristotelian tradition.

Of the four principles of inquiry which Descartes enumerates towards the end of the second part of the *Discourse on Method*, the first states the need of going back to the self-evident, to what presents itself so clearly and distinctly to the mind that there is no occasion for doubt. The second is a principle of analysis, the necessity of discriminating the aspects of a subject and the factors in a situation in order to arrive at what is really clear and distinct. The third is a principle of reconstruction, supposing that the clear, distinct and self-evident has been discovered; in the light of the primary evidences the more complex and difficult is gradually to be made intelligible and to gain a derivative clearness and evidence. The fourth is simply a principle of adequacy, making sure that nothing relevant has been omitted.

The resemblance of these principles to the proposed systematization of knowledge in the *Posterior Analytics* is obvious. Like Aristotle, Descartes supposes that it is possible to discover self-evident data and that there can be derivative evidence or valid inference from primary data. His originality is to apply this scheme to the criticism of what we usually take to be the contents of human experience.

III

The natural question which we first ask about Descartes' primary evidence, the *cogito*, is the meaning of *ergo* in *cogito, ergo sum*. But the meaning of *ergo* here depends on the meanings of *cogito* and *sum*. *Cogito* does not raise much difficulty. Descartes plainly means that experience certainly occurs, however doubtful we may be what it is that we experience. We may be perceiving or imagining, subject to dream or hallucination, but in any case something is occurring which Descartes describes as cogitation but which, on account of the customary intellectual connotation of cogitation in English, might be better called by some vague and neutral word such as "experience".

What, then, is the self which Descartes declares to be evidently revealed by any and every experience? The emphasis is not on the permanence of the self, for a single moment of experience is supposed to be sufficient to reveal it. Descartes is not, therefore, asking the same sort of question about the self as Hume was to ask. Nevertheless, he says that the *cogito* showed him that he was a substance whose whole essence or nature was to think and which, consequently, was not necessarily located in space or dependent on a body. Hence *sum* is not simply the abstraction of the subject-element from the verb-element in *cogito*; it is more like the abstraction of the verb-element from the object-element. The object-element in experience is not initially clear and distinct, but the fact of experience is undeniable. Thus *sum* isolates what is clear and distinct in the total situation described by *cogito*.

But, of course, the reference to substance indicates that it does more than this. When we reflect on what is clear and distinct in the situation of experience—and this is precisely the experiencing itself—Descartes holds that we recognize the self as an experient which is, so to say, a variable in relation to the contents of its experience, and which is essentially nothing else but an experient or mind. The *ergo* which unites *cogito* and *sum* is, therefore, obviously not a sign of syllogistic inference. Descartes is not saying: *Quod cogitat est; atqui cogito; ergo sum.* He is saying rather that, when we isolate what is clear and distinct in experience, which is the experiencing, we can at once see that this is a fundamental and independent variable which corresponds with what we mean by the self as mind. The *ergo* signifies an abstraction followed by a recognition of the nature of the clear and distinct element which we have isolated in reflection.

Three criticisms may be offered. First, can we thus at once isolate a general notion of experience which is entirely indifferent to what is experienced? No doubt experience can be used to cover perceiving, thinking, imagining, dreaming and so forth, but in such a use the term seems to be incurably vague. It does not appear that we can arrive at a clear and distinct notion without going back to that which is primary in experience and to which other sorts of event described as experience are relative. That is, the experience of being aware of something is clear and distinct but experience in general is not. Would not Descartes have done better and more in accordance with his own principles in isolating the notion of awareness and asking of what we can be really aware?

Secondly, the notion of experience isolated from real or possible objects seems to be merely an abstraction, a logically and grammatically incomplete expression. We have suggested that Descartes' conception of the thinking self is like the conception of a variable, but a variable has determinate reality only in its instances. Is our notion of the self as subject really of this kind? At least we may suggest that the Aristotelian conception of substance as a subject of potentialities is rather more subtle and that, even though on an Aristotelian view substances do not exist without actual attributes, they are a real factor in the metaphysical structure of reality in a way that a mere variable is not.

Thirdly, is our primary experience of the self an experience of the self simply as mind? Descartes may here be accused of offending against his fourth principle, the principle of adequacy. For when we reflect on human experience in the concrete, we are surely aware of ourselves as embodied things having sensations and perceptions and so forth. The Cartesian analysis might commend itself as permitting no doubt about our spirituality and natural immortality, but this is a spurious consolation. There is no normal human experience of the self which is not an experience of an embodied self, and man's survival after death is not self-evident but needs proof. The Cartesian approach to man, with a self-evident mind but no self-evident body, is lop-sided both in itself and in its consequences. This unfortunate aspect of Descartes' thought has, however, perpetuated itself persistently. In our own century, for example, G. E. Moore's primary notion of the self is still that of a disembodied awareness.

It is true, nevertheless, that in some sense the *cogito* is primary in a theory of knowledge. We must begin in some way with the undeniable fact of experience. But the implications which Descartes drew from the *cogito* are in many respects faulty. An embodied self having sensations and reflectively aware both of itself and of them is more adequate to the facts of experience than the disembodied variable which is the Cartesian self.

IV

From the Cartesian point of view, however, the initial situation was that of an experient self whose sole unmistakable object was itself. Of other things it had representative ideas, which for Descartes as for everyone else would seem to indicate the presence of other persons and things, but whose objective validity had to be justified. It seems fairly clear that the doctrine of representative ideas offers an insoluble problem. If we only know ideas or images of things and have no direct acquaintance with the things of which they purport to be ideas or images, it does not appear possible ever to discover whether they represent these things accurately or even whether the things exist at all. Even the more subtle form in which the doctrine reappears in Kant, who explicitly abdicates any claim to decide whether appearance resembles reality, is difficult to interpret in any plausible way. The cruder Cartesian doctrine of representative ideas manifests the absurdity in the clearest light.

But the origin of this doctrine is worth exploring. It is not Aristotelian, although it may well be connected with the controversy, mentioned by Aristotle, whether like knows like or unlike knows unlike. This difference is made the leading division of theories of sensation by Aristotle's immediate disciple, Theophrastus.

> The various opinions concerning sense perception, when regarded broadly, fall into two groups. By some investigators it is ascribed to similarity, while by others it is ascribed to contrast: Parmenides, Empedocles and Plato attribute it to similarity; Anaxagoras and Heraclitus attribute it to contrast.[1]

Aristotle himself had dealt with the question in accordance with his principles about acting and being acted upon; before being stimulated, the sense-faculty is unlike its object but becomes like it through stimulation and in the act of perception.[2] If we recall also the Aristotelian axiom that knowledge is a reception of the form of the object without its matter, we are justified in stating generally that he held the subject to be able to know by being made in some way like its object.

Nevertheless, Aristotle is quite certain that what we know, in perception for example, is the object and not an image of it. The theory of a knowledge of the external world through

---

[1] Theophrastus, *De Sensibus, I*: trans. *apud* G. M. Stratton. *Theophrastus and the Greek Physiological Psychology before Aristotle*, London, 1917, p. 67.
[2] Aristotle, *De Anima*, II, v, 417a, 19–21.

a reception of images from external objects is one which we find rather in the atomists, such as Democritus and Epicurus. It was they who spoke of effluxes and images (ἀπόῤῥοιαι, εἴδωλα) as thrown off by objects and making contact with the senses.

This image theory of cognition, however, seems to have had some part in the eclectic stock of notions which were common to late Hellenistic philosophy and to have been transmitted to the Middle Ages. For the medieval doctrine of intentional species vacillates rather uneasily between an Aristotelian and an Epicurean interpretation. Stimulated by means of a *species impressa*, the subject produces an act of awareness whose permanent result is a *species expressa* which can be recalled in imagination or memory. On an authentic Aristotelian interpretation the species is in either case *id quo obiectum cognoscitur*, not *id quod cognoscitur*, and natural realism is preserved. But the common view of the species as an image makes it very difficult to think of it except as *id quod cognoscitur*, an immediate object by means of which the external object is somehow attained. When Peter Aureoli (*d.* 1321–2) and Peter of Ailly (1350–1420) tell us that God could produce an incorrigible illusion of an external world by creating the species which we now have without having created the external world itself, they are evidently thinking of species which might have an existence and quasi-objectivity of their own. Equally, when Durandus and Ockham reject intentional species, they are obviously intending to preserve natural realism by excluding any image between the percipient and the external object. Thus, of course, they are faced with the embarrassment of leaving perception as a brute fact without explanation.

Much of the difficulty was evidently due to the lack of any clear distinction between the occurrence of sensation and the perception of an external object. It is important to realize that this distinction was not adequately made by anyone earlier than Reid in the eighteenth century. With the aid of this distinction it is easy to see that sensations and images are in themselves objects of consciousness which combine reality with subjectivity in the same way. The perception of an external object which may accompany a sensation and the supposal of an external object which may accompany an image are different functions of mind. But when sensation and perception are confused, we are faced with the dilemma of either accepting perception as a brute fact or explaining it by some transmission of images which it becomes difficult to exclude as objects prior to the perceptual act and compromising its validity.

For Descartes, then, the intentional species had become a representative idea, and he was only too well aware, with Peter Aureoli and Peter of Ailly, that on such a view we might, absolutely speaking, have all the representative ideas which we now have without there being any external world at all. Whatever we may think of his attempt to overcome this difficulty we can at least understand from the history of thought how he came to be faced by it.[1]

Since Descartes' assumptions are thus faulty, we need not detain ourselves by examining in detail how he thought to substantiate a belief in the external world. Having arrived at the existence of God, mainly on the basis of the ontological argument, he asserts that God could not deceive us by implanting in us an incorrigible tendency to believe what was not true. But our impression of an external world of extended things in motion was so clear and distinct that ordinary human thinking had no option but to accept this as fact. It was different with the specific sense-qualities of colour, sound, taste, smell and the rest. These were so comparatively vague and variable that we could easily come to regard them as subjective experiences accompanying our awareness of matter in motion. Hence, while the specific sense-qualities were affections of the subject, the reality of the world of matter in motion must be upheld. We observe,

---

[1] Although our historical information is now greater, it is still useful to consult on this subject Hamilton's dissertation in his edition of Reid: Note M: "On the Doctrine of Species."

by the way, that the specific sense-qualities have thus ceased to be representative ideas, for they represent nothing external. This breach in the doctrine might have suggested a reconsideration of the doctrine of representative ideas in general, but Descartes does not take up the point and the doctrine remains as an embarrassment for Locke.

v

Another question remains, however, which is important for our purposes. Was Descartes' project a quest for clearness or a quest for certainty? The clearness and distinctness of an idea is said to constitute the evidence on account of which we accept it as genuinely representative of the real. There seems to be some confusion here. Allowance must be made for the situation in which we are quite sure that we are aware of something although the experience is anything but clear and distinct. Alice's reaction to reading "Jabberwocky" is an extreme case. "Somehow it seems to fill my head with ideas—only I don't exactly know what they are!"

A philosopher embarks on the Cartesian quest when he finds that the language of common sense is rather more like "Jabberwocky" than seems altogether healthy. But his subsequent thinking continues to presuppose common experience. As Professor G. E. Moore was later to emphasize, there is a sense in which the existence of trees and rocks, chairs and tables, possesses a certainty prior to philosophy and independent of it. It is true that this is a progressively vanishing sense, but it never completely vanishes, or philosophy would have nothing left to work upon. What trees and rocks, chairs and tables, *are*, whatever we may propose to say *about* them, is thrown into question, but they continue to be there as the subject-matter of our questions.

The point may be expressed in another way, also with reference to Lewis Carroll, by considering the suggestion that we do not really know the Snark at all until we discover that it is a Boojum. This plainly will not do. We must know that there is a Snark if we are to begin hunting it, although in another sense we know nothing about it while all Boojum-sentences are doubtful. The philosopher's job is to hunt the Snark by all possible means until he is able to assert a Boojum-sentence. That he will then softly and suddenly vanish away is an opinion of Wittgenstein which we shall have to consider later.

The Cartesian project should, then, be construed primarily as a quest for clearness rather than as a quest for certainty. Philosophy is neither an apologetic for common sense nor a disintegration of common sense. It seeks understanding at what a philosopher cannot help calling a deeper level. That is, the philosopher examines what is taken for granted in ordinary thinking; he uncovers the presuppositions of common experience in the hope of arriving at what is logically primary, and of reinterpreting common experience in terms of this. He should be able to pursue his task without either succumbing to a nervous dread that the world will disappear in the process or putting up a bluff to support what is vague and hasty in the formulations of common sense.

At his best Descartes was trying to do precisely this. He was trying to discover ultimate data and to understand the world in terms of them. If his final argument for the reality of the external world looks to some extent like a bluff, this is because his initial analysis was in several respects defective and called for a desperate remedy. Perhaps, indeed, his argument is not as ineffective as it is unusual. A theist whose theism is a logical consequence of the acknowledgment of the finiteness and contingency of the self may well argue that his creator would not leave him in irremediable error or doubt about the general character of experience. But it is certainly to be questioned whether a recourse to theological considerations is necessary at this stage. The successors of Descartes were right both in supposing that his type of inquiry had come to stay and in looking for a more natural kind of solution of the problems involved in it.

CHAPTER II

The British Empiricists and the Narrowing of the Field

I

Most of the French Cartesians seem to have deserved Leibniz's reproach that they were mere commentators on their master and did little but construct dogmatic systems on foundations which they took for granted. It was left to the British empiricists to criticize in its turn and to renew Descartes' own criticism of the foundations of experience. Whether these philosophers fully deserve to be described as empiricists might be questioned, for human experience seems on a broad commonsense view to be a rich and complex field, whereas the empiricists in their development from Locke to Hume appear to make it gradually more impoverished and schematic. It is indeed wholly pertinent to ask whether the empiricists were adequately empirical or true to the whole of experience. Nevertheless, they were governed by the intention of being faithful to the facts of experience and to these facts alone, and we have to try to understand how such an intention could lead in the end to the world of Hume.

Hobbes was a contemporary critic of Descartes, but he arrives at his materialistic system of the universe with such dogmatic rapidity that his gratuitous assumptions and omissions scarcely call for detailed comment. We may be permitted the rapid dogmatic comment that he is really interesting only as a political thinker. Locke, on the other hand, deserves to be taken seriously.

Although Locke devotes the first book of his *Essay* to a polemic against the Cartesian doctrine of innate ideas, he accepts the Cartesian approach to the problem of perception by the assumption of representative ideas. In the end, however, as with Descartes, only the ideas of the primary qualities or quantitative factors turn out to resemble external reality; the ideas of the secondary qualities, the specific qualities of sensation, are held not to resemble the qualities of things but to be affections of the sentient subject. This conclusion might well have warned Locke as well as Descartes of the dubious character of the initial assumption.

In fact it was the merit of Berkeley to dissipate this muddle and to reject the theory of representative ideas altogether. For Berkeley sensations simply are what they are; they neither are nor purport to be representations of anything else. In this respect Berkeley was more of a natural realist than either Descartes or Locke; it was his further assumption that the primary qualities are nothing but features of sensation which made him an immaterialist.

The word "idea" as used by Berkeley implies, then, that sensations belong to the sentient subject but not that they are pictures of anything. Hume uses "idea" in a third sense as meaning images in their contrast with original impressions. Thus there are the primary impressions of sensation and the secondary impressions of feeling, with the ideas which correspond with each class when they are revived in imagination or memory. But Hume no more than Berkeley puts the question of the origin of knowledge in terms of the doctrine of representative ideas.

II

What, then, are primary data of experience for Locke, Berkeley and Hume? Locke's primary data are the ideas of sensation and the ideas of reflection. Neglecting what is usually called internal sensation, Locke thinks of the ideas of sensation as purporting to resemble external objects; the discovery that the primary qualities can really be attributed to external objects, whereas the secondary qualities cannot, goes beyond the field of the given. The ideas of reflection are less properly called ideas in Locke's terminology, for they are a genuinely intuitive awareness of the operations of our own minds.

Although the ideas of relation result from comparing things together, they are logically data, for they are not inferred but observed. Among such observed relations Locke includes the relation of cause and effect, for he states that "we cannot but observe that . . . qualities and substances begin to exist; and that they receive this their existence from the due application and operation of some other being".[1] The ideas of substances are derived partly from observation of the constant concomitance of a group of qualities but are not wholly data of experience, for the unitary subject of such a group of qualities is not observed but inferred. For, "not imagining how these simple ideas can subsist by themselves, we accustom ourselves to suppose some *substratum* wherein they do subsist, and from which they do result; which therefore we call 'substance' ".[2] The unity of the self, however, is a fact of experience for Locke, for it consists in the continuity of consciousness and is independent of any speculations concerning a substance underlying conscious activity.

Berkeley's initial data consist of the ideas of sensation and of the consciousness of the self. "I know or am conscious of my own being; and that *I myself* am not my ideas, but somewhat else, a thinking, active principle that perceives, knows, wills, and operates about ideas." This knowledge of the active self is said to be "immediate or intuitive".[3] Berkeley emphasizes that the awareness of the self is of a different kind from our awareness of the data of sensation. We have not strictly an idea of the self, for ideas are passive and inert whereas the awareness of the self is essentially of an active principle. One aspect of the contrast between the

[1] *Essay on the Human Understanding*, bk. ii, ch. xxvi, § 1.
[2] Op. cit., bk. ii, ch. xxiii, § 1.
[3] Berkeley, *Third Dialogue between Hylas and Philonous*, ed. Campbell-Fraser, Oxford, 1901, pp. 450, 447–8.

spiritual and the material is precisely the opposition of active and passive. We may be said, then, to have a notion of the self rather than an idea, and it is possible to conceive of minds other than our own. But my own mind is the only mind of which I am immediately aware.

For Hume the data are the impressions and ideas of sensation and of feeling, together with certain relations which can be seen to subsist between these, but certainly not the relation of cause and effect, of which his destructive criticism is so familiar. There is no immediate awareness of things capable of persisting through time, or of a self which is anything other than the serial character of the impressions and ideas which make up the history of a mind. There is not even, therefore, the persistent variable of consciousness which was admitted by Locke as by Descartes.

III

Such being the data, we may make an equally brief comparison of what our authors arrive at from them. Locke says that "we have the knowledge of our own existence by intuition; of the existence of God by demonstration; and of other things by sensation". [1] But it is clear from what follows that our conviction of the existence of other things has to be supported by inference. Psychologically, no doubt, we begin to believe in the external world before we explicitly reason about it, and that is presumably what Locke means by attributing this belief to sensation. It is, however, belief rather than knowledge that he ought to have attributed, even in this vague way, to sensation, for on his assumptions knowledge of the external world is a matter of explicit inference and even our spontaneous belief appears to be implicitly inferential.

The self of which Locke claims to be intuitively aware is, of course, the unity of consciousness; it does not include our embodiedness. For the demonstration of the existence of

---

[1] *Essay on the Human Understanding*, bk. iv, ch. ix, § 2.

God Locke rejects the ontological argument, together with Descartes' special suggestion of an innate idea of God implanted by him, but adheres to the causal or cosmological argument. Whether he presents this adequately need not concern us now.

Locke admits that the occurrence of ideas does not by itself prove the existence of an external world corresponding to them; they may be purely imaginary. But he thinks that we can discern cases in which our ideas are produced from without from cases in which our ideas are produced from within; that is, we can discern sensation from imagination. In cases of sensation, when our ideas are produced from without, we cannot but conceive of their causes as possessing the primary qualities of extension and solidity, although we need not suppose the secondary qualities to be resemblances of external objects; it is enough to suppose that bodies have the power of stimulating these specific sorts of sensation in our minds. Hence we have all the evidence that we need for the existence of the external world, for "the confidence that our faculties do not herein deceive us is the greatest assurance we are capable of concerning the existence of material things".[1]

Locke is not unaware of the naivety of his argument and concedes that it lacks the undeniability of both intuition and strict demonstration. He is content, however, at this point, with commonsense pragmatism. But to his honour it should be mentioned that the germ of a more interesting conception is present in his discussion of solidity as distinct not only from pure space but from sensible hardness. Although he says that the idea of solidity is received by touch, yet the fact that "it arises from the resistance which we find in body to the entrance of any other body into the place it possesses till it has left it"[2] suggests that it is rather more than a transitory quality of sensation. It might perhaps have been well if Locke had followed up the implications of this line of thought.

[1] Op. cit., bk. iv, ch. xi, § 3. [2] Op. cit., bk. ii, ch. iv, § 1.

For an explanation of what we mean by the material world Berkeley seeks to persuade us that it is unnecessary to go beyond the data. Material things simply are collections of what he calls ideas; they are, in more modern language, systems of sense-data. The existence of other minds, however, is reached by inference. The universal system of sense-data evidently possesses a stability and consistency which it does not owe to its fragmentary manifestations in finite minds. There must, therefore, be a universal mind which determines the whole system of sense-data and adapts it to the needs of finite minds with a wisdom and benevolence which entitles us to regard the sense-data which make up the actual material world as a natural revelation of God, a language in which God speaks to us.

The existence of other finite minds is inferred from the observation of changes in the material world which imply finite rational activity, the prosecution of particular ends. "From motions, therefore, you infer a mover or cause," says Euphranor to Alciphron, "and from reasonable motions (or such as appear calculated for a reasonable end) a rational cause, soul or spirit."[1] In the case of finite minds, however, the value of such evidence does not appear to exceed probability, for Philonous remarks that "it is granted we have neither immediate evidence nor a demonstrative knowledge of the existence of other finite spirits".[2] Berkeley does not seem to have been troubled by this lack of complete evidence any more than Locke was troubled by the lack of complete evidence for the existence of an external world in general. An implicit pragmatism came to the rescue in both cases.

Hume's world begins and ends with impressions and ideas. For demonstrative reasoning is based upon relations which follow at once from the nature of their terms. These are "resemblance, contrariety, degrees in quality, and pro-

---

[1] Berkeley, *Alciphron*, iv, 4, ed. Campbell-Fraser, Oxford, 1901, p. 159.
[2] Berkeley, *Third Dialogue between Hylas and Philonous*, ed. Campbell-Fraser, p. 450.

portions in quantity or number".[1] The first three of these kinds of relation are discoverable by intuition, so that only the fourth gives rise to deductive knowledge. The deductive sciences are exclusively mathematical.

In the realm of concrete fact we reason in terms of cause and effect. This does not produce knowledge in any objective sense, for it is reducible to expectations based on association. Such expectations are frequently fulfilled, but there is no reason to show that they should or must be fulfilled. Still less can they introduce us to any new sort of object. "Since nothing is ever present to the mind but perceptions, and since all ideas are derived from something antecedently present to the mind; it follows, that 'tis impossible for us so much as to conceive or form an idea of any thing specifically different from idea and impressions."[2] Hence a belief in external objects is simply the supposition of impressions and ideas which do not, or have not yet, entered into our experience.

IV

When we reflect on the work of Locke, Berkeley and Hume, we may first observe that Berkeley represents an advance on Locke in virtue of his total rejection of representative ideas. The issue is no longer confused by the insoluble pseudo-problem of comparing the ideas of things with the things of which they purport to be ideas. Sights, sounds, tastes, smells and tactile data are acknowledged on reflection to be real in their own right although it seems equally clear that they are objects of consciousness in the strict sense, affections of the sentient subject. If this is so, it has a contemporary moral also, for it means that we cannot avoid a recognition of sense-data as a specific class of object.

The ground having thus been cleared, the logical force of Berkeley's conclusions in relation to his premises must also be admitted. If what is initially given consists simply

[1] Hume, *Treatise of Human Nature*, bk. i, pt. iii, § i., ed. Selby-Bigge, Oxford, 1928, p. 70.
[2] Ibid., bk. i, pt. ii, § 6, ed. Selby-Bigge, p. 67.

of the experient self and its sensations, there is no reason to suppose that material things are anything more than systems of actual and possible sense-data. When Bertrand Russell, in our own day, proposed a similar theory, he was following the same principle of logical economy as Berkeley.

But is it true that nothing is initially given but the experient self and its sensations? Can the feeling of being embodied be interpreted wholly in terms of the specific sense-qualities? The apprehension of space is usually attributed, mainly at least, to sight and touch. Berkeley himself, however, in his *New Theory of Vision*, had pointed out that although visual and tactile extension come to be almost inextricably associated, they are in themselves quite distinct. Berkeley maintained that visual extension has in itself only two dimensions and that no sort of awareness of distance is primitively available to the eye. Visual distance is an imaginative supplement to the visual datum due to its amalgamation with tactile space. This opinion of Berkeley has often been contradicted; it is often held that the visual datum already has a certain character of outness from the eye. Yet a phenomenological reflection suggests that there is much to be said for Berkeley's view of the nature of vision in itself; I can only say that my own reflection leads me to agree with him.

We have still to ask whether he was right in attributing the primitive awareness of true three-dimensional space to touch. Here it may well be that he did not carry his discriminations far enough. For tactile qualities, the feelings of hardness and softness, roughness and smoothness, do not seem in themselves to have a spatial character. They are very closely associated with our awareness of space, no doubt, but is this not because we are immediately aware of an embodied self as the bearer of these sensations? And, although this awareness of the embodied self is clearest in connection with tactile sensations diffused over the organism, is there not a dim awareness of an embodied self in relation to all sensations as the bearer of them? If this is so, the data of consciousness consist not merely of an experient self and its sensations but of an embodied self and its sensations. Although we could have no awareness of ourselves apart from the stimulus of sensation, our awareness of ourselves sensing is more than a pure awareness of sense-data.

The suggestion is now open that the material world is not a construction out of sense-data but that, along with the primitive consciousness of an embodied self, there is a primitive perception of other bodies in dynamic relation with our own. These bodies we naturally regard as stimulating our sensations but not as consisting of sense-data or possessing in themselves any qualities like the specific qualities of sensation. Locke's distinction of fundamental solidity or occupation of volume from specific tactile qualities, such as hardness and softness, roughness and smoothness, is here to the point. Sir William Hamilton develops this theme in order to complete Reid's account. For Reid made a clear distinction between the consciousness of sensation and the perception of external objects and declared that "if Nature had given us nothing more than impressions made upon the body, and sensations in our minds corresponding to them, we should, in that case, have been merely sentient, but not percipient beings".[1] For the root of perception, however, Reid falls back vaguely on a natural instinct which makes an awareness of the external world accompany the experience of sensation. It was the merit of Hamilton to have found the root of perception in the inseparable awareness of an embodied self and of other bodies in dynamic contact with it.[2]

We may perhaps conclude that, although Berkeley's logic is forcible, his premises are inadequate. His system has the attraction of a clear and economical theory worked out with a praiseworthy measure of logical rigour. No philosopher is likely to suppose, with Dr. Johnson, that he can be refuted by kicking a stone. So far from denying the material world, he gave the best explanation of it compatible with his

[1] *Inquiry into the Human Mind*, ch. vi, § xxi, Edinburgh, 1862, p. 187.
[2] Cf. Hamilton's Note D.: "Distinction of the Primary and Secondary Qualities of Body," in his edition of Reid.

premisses. But the common man's objection is not altogether
without foundation, for Berkeley's premisses omit precisely
our primitive experience of the corporeal as such in our own
organisms and in the bodies with which we come into
contact.

v

Due tribute should also be paid to Berkeley for his
notion of the self as essentially active, for he was here well
on the way to the recovery of a feasible conception of substance. Locke's view of substance as an unknown somewhat
which served as a support of observable qualities was an
obvious invitation to a more economical thinker to abolish
the support and resolve the notion of substance into some
sort of systematic or customary association of the observable
qualities themselves. This, of course, is exactly what Hume
did with the self, making it into a mere series of impressions
and ideas. Berkeley had given regrettably little development to his notion of the self, but Hume can hardly be
excused for having ignored it altogether.

We must ask ourselves how Hume came to so impoverished
a view of reality, for the Humian tendency is still so much
with us that this question is relevant to a great deal of modern
British philosophy. In the first place, Hume seems to have
been unable to notice persistent data. For the self as agent
and the self as embodied are persistent data in our experience.
But it seems to have required a change to wake Hume up and
make him notice that anything was present. All that he
could bring himself to admit were the more superficial and
changing factors in experience.

Secondly, Hume seems to have expected every element in
the given to be a separate concrete fact. He complains that
he cannot find any distinct impression of a continuous self.

> It must be some one impression, that gives rise to every real
> idea. But self or person is not any one impression, but that to
> which our several impressions and ideas are suppos'd to have

a reference. If any impression gives rise to the idea of self, that impression must continue invariably the same, thro' the whole course of our lives; since self is suppos'd to exist after that manner. But there is no impression constant and invariable. Pain and pleasure, grief and joy, passions and sensations succeed each other, and never all exist at the same time. It cannot therefore, be from any of these impressions, or from any other, that the idea of self is deriv'd; and consequently there is no such idea.[1]

But obviously the self is to be found in its experiences and not apart from them. The identical self is not a separate atomic fact but is to be discovered by an analytic reflection upon our experience as not less real than the changing contents of experience. Neither the changing experiences nor the unchanging experient are concrete in isolation; concrete fact contains them both and thinking discriminates them.

But, of course, any conception of a revealing activity of thought is alien to Hume. This can be illustrated by his views on the classical question of universals, where he echoes Locke with a more sceptical undertone. Locke had thought that there must be something which we could call a universal concept but that it must be a vague idea which somehow stood in our minds as representative of a class of things like it. Hume in effect says the same but stresses the fact that any such idea must really be a particular, so that the theory of universal concepts cannot literally be upheld. He claims to be echoing Berkeley, but Berkeley's second thoughts at least were more penetrating than anything in Locke or Hume on the subject, for he says that "it must be acknowledged that a man may consider a figure merely as triangular, without attending to the particular qualities of the angles, or relations of the sides".[2]

This is all we need or should demand. There are no universal concepts in the sense of objects which are universal, for

[1] *Treaties of Human Nature*, bk. i, pt. iv, § 6, ed. Selby-Bigge, pp. 251–2.
[2] *Principles of Human Knowledge*, Intro., § 16 (added in 2nd ed.).

every real object is individual. But there are such activities as thinking abstractly and universally, and these activities are revelatory of the real. We can by thinking discern different factors within a single concrete datum, and we can recognize genuine similarities between different data. It is foolish to suppose that we can do justice to experience without thinking about it, but in the last resort that appears to have been precisely Hume's erroneous supposition. Hence it is difficult to share the respect which later British philosophy has generally accorded to him.

The fundamental criticism of Locke, Berkeley and Hume is, therefore, that they were not empirical enough. Their views of the contents of experience were inadequate. While Berkeley is far more profound and far more rigorously logical than either Locke or Hume, even his outlook is vitiated by a neglect of the experience of being embodied and in contact with other bodies. In order to transcend the limitations of the classical empiricists we need to take into account, as only Berkeley did, the experience of the self as active and acted upon and, as none of the empiricists did, the experience of the self as embodied. In any case we need a clearer conception than any of them had of the scope and achievement of thinking as contrasted with merely sensing and imagining. This, of course, leads us both logically and historically to Kant's problems.

CHAPTER III

Kant and the Scope of Thinking

I

KANT was convinced that passive sensation by itself would be the meaningless succession of impressions and ideas to which Hume had reduced it. He also assumed rather rashly that the material of sensation did not intrinsically manifest features by which the mind could be stimulated to make perceptual judgments and to build up an ordered view of the external world. But he was equally convinced that experience never really had the chaotic character attributed to it by Hume. Hence he was constrained to believe that the objective world as we experience it was partly the creation of forms of sensibility and categories of understanding inherent in the mind itself. The world of experience was, therefore, a world of things as they had to appear to us, whose relationship to things as they were in themselves remained inevitably problematic.

While such a theory provokes resistance by turning the relation of thought to fact topsy-turvy, thought determining its object rather than the object determining thought, there are other considerations which may make it seem not unplausible. When we take a broad view, for example, of history or geography, we seem to have a picture of the world in space and time which we hope to approximate to what the world really is and was, but which remains indefinitely corrigible. The historical fact in its full exactness, *wie es· eigentlich gewesen,* is beyond our grasp.

The position in the physical sciences has a certain similarity. We interpret the facts in terms of hypothetical entities and try to fit the facts into hypothetical generalizations, but our interpretations and generalizations remain indefinitely corrigible. The pure physical fact as it is transcends the knowledge of the physicist.

It has traditionally been supposed that philosophy or metaphysics yields a genuine knowledge of the real as such. But this claim is somewhat tarnished by the uncertainties and contradictions of philosophers. May it not be that all human knowledge is a matter of probability and approximation, never going beyond the thing as it appears to us to the thing as it really is in itself?

In that case the business of the philosopher is transformed. He must renounce the overweening ambition of traditional metaphysics and study instead the general conditions of human knowledge. He must ask what are the categories and maxims which thought employs in seeking order and intelligibility, and how it should employ them. Only thus will a really critical philosophy be possible.

On these broad lines Kant's proposals seem not unreasonable. But the fundamental objection, that they overturn the whole notion of knowing, persists. While the vast mass of what we should call our views and opinions remain in the sphere of probability and approximation, it appears that all probabilities and approximations rest ultimately on a foundation, however humble and restricted, of a genuine knowledge of what is. Hence Kantian phenomenalism will not do as a fundamental and universal theory of knowledge. To substantiate this, however, entails a more detailed kind of criticism which will attach itself to Kant's more analytical approach to his theory. We find this approach in his study of the proposition.

II

Kant evidently accepted in a rather crude form the view that a proposition imports an identity of subject and predicate. On that view it would seem at first that the only propositions which are self-evident and can be seen to be true *a priori* or independently of experience are those which are analytic, that is, those in which the predicate is part of the meaning of the subject. Correspondingly, synthetic propositions, those in which the predicate stands outside the meaning of the subject, would appear to be lacking in self-evidence in abstraction and knowable only *a posteriori* or through experience. In his early dogmatic period, in which he was dependent on Leibniz and Wolff, Kant does indeed seem to have supposed that the propositions of metaphysics, as of logic and mathematics, were not only *a priori* but analytic.

When, in the preface to the *Prolegomena*, Kant describes most fully how Hume woke him up, he refers to Hume's examination of causality as showing him that causal propositions were not analytic. Once he even slips back into the usage in accordance with which the *a priori* is identified with the analytic, for he states that Hume demonstrated the impossibility of reason's excogitating the causal relationship *a priori*. This is in obvious verbal conflict with the doctrine that causal propositions are synthetic *a priori*, but it may serve as a preliminary warning that synthetic *a priori* propositions are not *a priori* in precisely the same sense as are analytic propositions.

Hume criticized both specific causal propositions, in which this is said to be the cause of that, and what he took to be the metaphysical principle of causality, the principle that whatever begins to exist has a cause. Hume could not admit any objectively necessary connection either between beginning to exist and being caused or between any thing or event thought to be a cause and the distinct thing or event thought to be an effect. Although Kant does not clearly distinguish these two questions, he evidently admits Hume's criticism in both cases in the sense that he admits Hume to have demonstrated that such propositions are not analytic.

But, says Kant, such propositions are plainly necessary, in the sense that we cannot organize our experience and make it intelligible without them. Nor did Hume fail to recognize that common sense could not do without them. Hence Hume's first adversaries, among whom he mentions Reid, Oswald, Beattie and Priestley, went astray when they made the indispensability of causal notions the burden of their attack. Here Hume had no quarrel with them. The real difficulty was that his attempt to account for these notions on a pure *a posteriori* basis, the theory of expectations based on customary association, was manifestly too weak to sustain the weight that we cannot avoid laying upon them. The problem, therefore, was—granted both the absolute indispensability of causal propositions and Hume's demonstration that they were not analytic—to give a satisfactory account of their origin and place in human thinking.

Kant describes the course of reflection by which he was led to see that similar considerations were applicable to other questions in metaphysics. It was necessary, for example, he assumed, to interpret the world in terms of substance and attribute; but he judged this relation to be neither purely *a priori* and analytic nor simply presented in experience and *a posteriori*. Metaphysics was neither a purely experimental science nor a pure analysis of concepts. Its categories and principles had to be explained in some third and hitherto unknown way.

That is the essential background of the doctrine of the synthetic *a priori* proposition. Such a proposition is not purely *a priori* in the way that a mere analysis of concepts is, nor is it a mere registration of presented fact. It is synthetic, for the predicate is not contained in the subject, and it arises only in connection with experience. Indeed, as is shown at length in the empirical deduction of the categories, it may be said to be suggested by experience. But it is *a priori* in the sense that it is not simply given in experience but represents the exercise of our organizing thinking power upon the material of experience in accordance with the inherent laws of thought.

Kant also, of course, tells us that he came to see how synthetic *a priori* thinking was involved in any genuinely scientific knowledge. Logic was not psychological description of how people actually reason but laid down rules for reasoning which transcended experience and were never perfectly verified in it. Geometry became a science when the Greek geometers realized that their business was not simply with the approximations to circles and triangles which are to be found in the physical world, but that they could achieve precision only by considering the ideal circle and the ideal triangle which do not really exist. Kant found a similar *a priori* element in arithmetic, but his view of arithmetic is somewhat peculiar and is never made very clear. He seems to have thought of numbers as products of the operations of counting and of each number as being a group with a distinctive character. Hence numbering may also be thought of as a way of moulding reality to the exigencies of human thinking.

It is also a little startling when Kant attributes the advance of the physical sciences since Galileo to a similar importation of the *a priori*, for we might well think that a more exact and detailed observation of fact had much to do with it. But Kant is obviously not thinking of the observational stage of scientific inquiry; he is thinking of the stage of hypothesis and verification. An hypothesis is suggested by the facts but is not entailed by them; the process of verifying it is not reading it off from the facts but seeing whether the facts will fit in with it. In this way Kant is able to contrast Aristotelian physics as a mistaken attempt to discover physical laws intuitively with modern physics as a challenge to nature to answer the questions which the physicist frames and puts to the facts.

The sciences, therefore, according to Kant, have made real progress only when their practitioners have abandoned the naïve hope of extracting them, as it were, ready-made from their material and have begun to make systematic use of the constructive powers of thought to impose form and shape on the material provided by experience. A similar Copernican revolution, he maintained, was needed in philosophy. This was really more like a revolution from Copernicus to Ptolemy than one from Ptolemy to Copernicus, for it consisted in subduing the world to the needs of human thought and making the universe revolve round man rather than man round the universe. The philosopher had to acknowledge and to describe systematically the *a priori* notions and principles which, on the occasion of experience, the mind produced from its own resources to make the syntheses by which we become aware of genuine objects and of order between objects. He had at the same time to recognize that, if this is the origin of human knowledge, its object consists of things as they appear to us and not of things as they are in themselves, and that, although our *a priori* notions and principles are the appropriate presuppositions of our experience, there is no reason to suppose that they would hold in respect of things in themselves. Hence the dual purpose of the *Critique of Pure Reason*: the positive aim of elucidating the *a priori* element in human knowledge and the negative aim of showing both the impossibility of thought without it and the erroneous consequences of extending its validity beyond phenomena to things in themselves.

III

The question of the *a priori* synthesis is in this way central to Kant's philosophy. In asking whether we have to accept his solution of it, we must evidently examine more carefully the nature of propositions in general. But, proceeding from the outworks to the centre, we may first ask whether the progress of the physical sciences really lends Kant the support which he claims. There is undoubtedly a stage in scientific thinking at which we are concerned with hypothetical relations between hypothetical entities, and this stage has become still more characteristic of physics since the time of Kant. To that extent he was a prophet. For there we have a genuine contrast of phenomena with things in themselves, a system of representations which is our best available means of understanding the physical facts but whose precise relation to the facts is beyond our grasp. For, if we could know what the physical facts were in themselves, our hypothetical systems would be redundant.

Nevertheless such systems are not built entirely in the air. They presuppose a primary observational phase of scientific inquiry in which we take note of such facts as are directly accessible to us and form the generalizations which these facts make probable. A good hypothesis is at least suggested by the general character of the facts which we want to explain, and receives some initial intelligibility and probability from this before we see whether it fits all the observed facts. We do not simply say: "Let us suppose" but: "This looks as if it might be so." And the need of proceeding in the physical sciences by means of tentative hypothesis and verification seems to result from the comparative opacity to intelligence manifested by the corporeal world rather than from the character of our minds. In short, probable and approximate generalizations and hypotheses are valuable only in so far as they are supported by observed facts. In Kantian terms, science begins with things in themselves although it has to build a phenomenal system upon them.

In the case of geometry it is true that perfect circles and triangles are creations of thought, but we should certainly not be able to think of them if we had no perception of spatial entities. It is only because we perceive things which are more or less circular or triangular that the conception of the perfect circle or triangle is suggested to us. Moreover, it is conceivable that a physical object should be perfectly circular or triangular even if we do not know that any actually is.

Arithmetic may be interpreted even more realistically. There are pairs and triads, and so forth, of instances of types of thing in nature. There simply are five chairs in my study, neither more nor less. To give an exact physical description of what it means to be a chair in my study would involve a complex system of spatial relations, but it is clearly possible in principle. A certain subjective appearance attaches to arithmetic because our choice of numerical groups is usually dictated by our human purposes and interests, but the world, as the poet reminds us, is itself full of a number of things.

Finally, if logic represents an ideal of reasoning, it may temperately be hoped that it is not an ideal which is never realized. In any case, it certainly presupposes reflection on reasoning as it actually takes place. At least, therefore, it does not look as if human knowledge is confined to phenomena, with the thing as it is in itself out of reach. Even if we eventually have recourse to the ideal, the probable or the hypothetical, our speculations would be baseless if they did not begin with observed facts. If Kant's theory of knowledge were justified, it would be in spite of what scientific procedure appears to be and not as a counterpart of it.

What, then, of Kant's main argument founded on his division of propositions? It can be agreed that there is a sense in which it is appropriate to speak of the identity of subject and predicate in a true proposition. That is, in a singular proposition, what is asserted in the predicate is an element in the concrete fact referred to in the subject. If the subject is taken as naming a fact, the predicate, whether attributive or relational, is a part of that fact as a concrete whole.

But the kind of proposition in which Kant was interested was the universal proposition. Here we must remember something which was not noticed in Kant's day, and that is that a universal proposition is not simple but complex. It states not a relation between subject and predicate as these are understood in a singular proposition, but an entailment relation between two predicates. "All S is P" means that if anything has a predicate P_1, it will also have the predicate P_2. If we want to apply the concept of identity to a universal proposition, we must look for it, not between ostensible subject and predicate, but between anything possessing the

49

predicate indicated by the ostensible subject and the character of entailing the ostensible predicate. If, for example, we say that anything which begins to exist is caused, we are not asserting any sort of identity between beginning to exist and being caused, but we are claiming to be able to see that it is part of the being of anything which begins to exist that it should be caused.

Kant's distinction between analytic and synthetic universal propositions is, therefore, transformed into a distinction between overt or latent tautological entailments and non-tautological entailments. That all red roses are red is an overt tautology in which only a logician could be interested. But a great deal of philosophy consists in uncovering latent tautologies or showing the truth of analytic propositions. There are many features of fact which on the commonsense level we know only vaguely and globally and which it is the task of philosophy to try to reveal clearly and distinctly. Such is the situation in which we ask what we really mean by saying that something is good or that a proposition is true. The persistent disputes between rival analyses show that this kind of analysis is informative although, if successful, it results in a conclusion which is seen to have been a latent tautology.

If, however, there is to be any fruitful inference in philosophy, philosophy must be able to provide major premises which are non-tautological entailments or synthetic *a priori* propositions in the Kantian sense. Hence Kant's distinction, mistaken though his view of its implications was, remains important, and it is important to see that what he calls a synthetic *a priori* proposition may as easily be self-evident as what he calls an analytic proposition. There is no ground for asserting that all entailments must be tautological. There is no ground for asserting that we are never able to see that anything which possesses one predicate must also possess another different from it. Kant, therefore, did not prove the impossibility of an ontology, a theory of being as it is in itself. For it is a gratuitous assumption to suppose that the elements of fact are presented to us without connection or relation.

IV

The possibility of metaphysics, on the other hand, can be established only by doing it. Kant made an unconscious contribution to ontology when, in criticizing the ontological argument, he pointed out that existence was not a predicate. This is evidently a metaphysical statement, for existence is a perfectly sound grammatical and logical predicate. There is no grammatical difficulty about sentences which state that things exist, and it is logically unexceptionable to ask whether there is in fact anything corresponding with some concept or combination of concepts. The import of the statement that existence is not a predicate is that in the order of being there is nothing prior to being itself; everything else presupposes being and is a form or way of being.

Here lies precisely the contrast between thinking as a logician and thinking as a metaphysician. In the logical order we begin with concepts and may or may not relate them to fact; in the ontological order we proceed in the reverse direction, beginning with being and examining the forms which it takes, forms which are reflected in our concepts. For the logician as such, being is the horizon to his conceptual field; for the metaphysician, concepts manifest the participation and limitation of being.

That Kant did not continue in this manner need not deter anyone else from doing so. His real influence, however, has obviously been to set up a massive deterrent to the pursuit of a metaphysic of being. When we survey the progress of philosophy from Descartes to Kant, we see how the basic problems appeared which are still with us. The Cartesian project of a critical theory of knowledge commanded the efforts of philosophers. While Descartes' initial data were inadequate to his purpose, the work of the later empirical philosophers resulted not in an enlargement of the data but in a still greater restriction of what was admitted to be given in experience. The power of thinking to make the world intelligible was equally restricted. Either thinking was confined to tautologies or it was granted a function of purely logical or linguistic construction which could not claim to be a genuine understanding of fact. These difficulties still pervade contemporary philosophy.

PART II

CONTEMPORARY PHILOSOPHY

CHAPTER IV

Moore, Russell and Sense-Data

I

THE rebirth of British empirical philosophy in the present century is rightly regarded as due to the work of Professor G. E. Moore and of Lord Russell. During the latter half of the nineteenth century a form of Hegelian idealism, of which F. H. Bradley was undoubtedly the most brilliant exponent, had become predominant at the universities. Its unexpectedly rapid decline was brought about by Moore's assaults, but Moore's own philosophy did not develop precisely as expected. The early Moore looked as if he were taking up once again, even if with greater exactness, the task of the Scottish school of common sense, but in his hands, and still more in those of Bertrand Russell, the new empiricism gradually showed a greater and greater tendency to revert to Hume. We must ask why this was so.

There is no doubt that Moore intended, and continued to intend, to take common sense as an unquestionable foundation. This is upheld as late as in his paper on the "Proof of an External World", published in 1939. The paper is really a statement that the existence of the external world needs no proof. For the "proof" that two human hands exist consists of "holding up my two hands, and saying, as I make a certain gesture with the right hand, 'Here is one hand' and adding, as I make a certain gesture with the left, 'and here is another'".[1]

[1] "Proof of an External World." (Annual Philosophical Lecture, British Academy, 1939), p. 25.

The procedure here is purely analytic. The consequent, that two human hands exist, is simply a part of what is assumed as evident in the antecedent.

While, however, Moore regards a vast number of propositions about the existence of material objects as thus evidently true, the general tenor of his writings on perception shows that nearly everything about *what* material objects are remains to be investigated. We know that the Snark is, but we have still to find out whether it is a Boojum or not. The hunt begins with analysis. The suggested proof of an external world is scarcely an informative analysis, whatever Moore may have supposed it to be, for the result is already explicit at the start; but Moore is quite clear that analytic thinking can be informative.

His principles on this matter are stated at the beginning of *Principia Ethica*, where he tells us what he is doing in asking what is meant by "good". An arbitrary verbal definition tells us how someone intends to use a word. A verbal definition of the kind to be found in dictionaries tells us how people generally use a word. But there is another kind of definition which is of greater importance for philosophy, and which corresponds with what logicians mean by real definition. "We may mean that a certain object, which we all of us know, is composed in a certain manner."[1] When we know the meaning of a word, we can go on to inquire into the nature of the range of objects referred to by it. This is an ontological analysis by which we may come to know clearly and distinctly what we previously knew only vaguely and globally.

Such an analysis cannot be indefinitely protracted. We must eventually arrive at conceptual elements which we can only point out as best we may. It is in this sense that Moore himself holds "good" to be indefinable and simply to be recognized in appropriate situations. This may suggest the amendment that a notion, without being intrinsically composite, may yet presuppose another notion to which it is

[1] *Principia Ethica*, Cambridge, 1903, p. 8.

essentially relative and through its relation to which it is to be understood and defined. In this way the notion of good, without being composite, may yet be definable in terms of the degree of fulfilment of a nature.

This is not the place, however, in which to enter into specific criticism of Moore's ethics; we want only to widen his conception of the definable. Let us say, then, that philosophical analysis has the task of making us know clearly and distinctly what we previously knew only vaguely and globally, and that it performs this task either by revealing the constituents of a notion which turns out to be complex or by exhibiting the essential relativity of a notion which turns out not to be primary and independent. This is a widening of Moore's view but not its negation. What he has to say about philosophical analysis remains true and important.

Moreover, his principles of method do justice to the possibility of fruitful inference by bringing out the nature of entailment. In the paper on "External and Internal Relations" in *Philosophical Studies* he points out with the utmost clearness that neither material nor formal implication as understood in the Russell-Whitehead logic corresponds with the usual sense in which one thing is said to be deducible from another. Material and formal implication are defined in terms of what happens in fact to be the case; one proposition materially implies another if it is not the case that the former is true and the latter false. But deducibility in the usual sense is an intelligible relation, a connection of meanings; one proposition entails another when we can see that the latter must follow from the former in virtue of their respective contents in any case.

Although the most obvious instances of entailment are tautologies, Moore is far from suggesting that all entailments are tautologous or analytic. When, in the latter part of *Principia Ethica*, he goes on from discussing the meaning of good to inquiring what sorts of thing or situation are good, he asks us to acknowledge that his indefinable character of

57

goodness attaches to a number of things in whose definition goodness is not included. That is to say, he asks us to recognize a number of synthetic entailments. Aesthetic enjoyment is good; personal affection is good. Such statements are not tautologous.

Hence Moore is to be appreciated not only for the meticulous care with which he conducts his inquiries but for having laid down under the headings of analysis and entailment ·sound principles of philosophical method. If his investigation of the knowledge of the external world is inconclusive, this is not on account of a defect of method. He begins promisingly enough in the paper on "The Refutation of Idealism" with the assertion that awareness presupposes its object and the denial that *esse est percipi* in the sense in which that maxim asserts the contrary. If Moore later confessed his dissatisfaction with this early essay, there is at least one obvious reason. For it is ostensibly directed against Berkeley, and Berkeley should not be accused of asserting *esse est percipi* in this sense. Berkeley meant rather that the specific sense-qualities could not be supposed to occur except in a sentient subject; nevertheless they were real as qualities of such a subject. That they were not ideal representations of some problematic object beyond themselves Berkeley was as much concerned to deny as Moore; indeed, there is much in common between Berkeley's ideas and Moore's own sense-data.

Moore's difficulty is to discern the relation between the data of sensation as revealed by philosophical analysis and the world of material objects as envisaged by common sense. Although his discussions of the various possible theories are admirable examples of exact thinking, they fail to arrive at any positive result because Moore has not provided himself with adequate data. His self is the pure disembodied awareness which Descartes introduced into philosophy with such lasting disastrous results; its objects are simply the specific sense-qualities. Since it is through the active embodied self that we find ourselves in contact with the material things, which we then recognize to be the sources of our sensations, the neglect of the active embodied self as a primitive datum necessarily entails an inconclusive theory of perception. Moore, therefore, remains a philosopher who denied himself the material required to carry out his chosen work, but there is a great deal to learn both from his precepts of method and from his example in their application.

II

If Moore has been one of the most sparing of philosophical writers, Bertrand Russell has been one of the most voluminous. In politics he is a vigorous surviving specimen of the late nineteenth-century radical. Since he has never been able to find any justification for his ethical and political views except that they are his personal preferences which he would like others to share, it is fortunate that they are liberal and humane, even if they are somewhat lacking in the sharp edges which a sound morality must surely display at times. His place along with Whitehead in the development of symbolic logic is secure. His masterpiece, if I may express a personal opinion, is his *Introduction to Mathematical Philosophy*, which contains a concentrated mass of clear thinking on the nature of number and does not lose itself, as *Principia Mathematica* may be thought to lose itself at times, in a mere manipulation of symbols which has little or no significance for the advance of thought or the understanding of fact.

For the point of view from which Russell approaches general philosophy he is obviously indebted to the lead given by Moore. His primary problem, like Moore's, was the relationship of sense-data to the commonsense world of persons and things, and he began by thinking that a sufficiently persistent application of philosophical analysis in Moore's manner would eventually arrive at a satisfactory solution. His Lowell Lectures on "Our Knowledge of the External World", published in 1914, were "an attempt to show, by means of examples, the nature, capacity, and limitations of the logical-analytic method in philosophy. This method", the preface continues, "has gradually, in the course of actual research, increasingly forced itself upon me as something perfectly definite, capable of embodiment in maxims, and adequate, in all branches of philosophy, to yield whatever objective scientific knowledge it is possible to obtain."

These are brave words, although Russell does not seem ever to have carried into effect the proposal to embody his method in maxims. One leading idea, however, emerges in the same preface when he states that he owes to Whitehead "the whole conception of the world of physics as a *construction* rather than an inference". The same remark would doubtless apply to the world of common sense, and here is one salient difference between Russell's enterprise and Moore's. Moore accepted as evident a distinction between the world of sense-data and the world of physical objects, and looked for the logical transition from one to the other. Russell's aim was to exhibit the world of physical objects as a construction out of sense-data.

Paradoxically enough, however, Russell abolished the constructor. No doubt it was tempting to dispense with Moore's factor of awareness, which was merely an inactive spectator of whatever might be supposed to enter as an object into consciousness. At any rate, the *Analysis of Mind* (1921) contains Russell's rejection of anything which might be called consciousness other than the simple occurrence of sense-data. Mind had to be analysed as one kind, and physical objects as another kind, of construction out of sense-data. Since sense-data were the whole reality of both, this philosophy could be called neutral monism.

The concept of mind was replaced by that of a private space within which a number of sense-data could occur in a certain unity at the same time. By what in commonsense language would be called moving or changing our point of view other groups of sense-data could be obtained. Members of some groups were found to fall into relation with members of other groups by a gradually greater resemblance or differentiation, as with the visual data obtained when we would normally say that we were approaching an object. Hence a public space could be constructed which contained all possible points of view arranged with their continuously changing degree of resemblance or difference. Minds were the points of view actually occupied, that is to say, the points of view at which sense-data were actually occurring.

Sense-data could also be ordered in another way. Those which resembled one another could be traced from various directions back to a source in the same public space. The source was a part of public space in which they did not occur although they occurred with greatest intensity all round it and with diminishing intensity at a distance from it. A physical object was a part of public space which was in this way a source of characteristic sense-data. These ideas are worked out in principle in the papers on "The Ultimate Constituents of Matter" and "The Relation of Sense-data to Physics" in *Mysticism and Logic,*

There could certainly be no more ingenious attempt than Russell's to build up a semblance of the world of common sense using no materials other than those allowed by Hume. For it will be clear that Russell's analysis of experience had brought him back to Hume's position. But the notion of constructions which have no constructor remains a difficulty. Minds and things are said to be logical constructions out of sense-data, but, if mind is itself a construction, it can hardly be also the constructor. The fact of language has still to be recognized, and those who followed Russell's route after him have tended to interpret logical constructions as linguistic constructions. Words have been assigned the necessary function of ordering and unifying the contents of experience. How talking constructs the talker now becomes the problem, and perhaps it is a problem which suggests rather strongly that something has gone wrong in the reasoning which leads up to it.

III

Russell has sometimes been accused of changing his mind unduly often, but it is a virtue to be discontented with what is plainly inadequate. At any rate the last systematic statement of his general views in *Human Knowledge* (1948) contains some interesting modifications of what he had hitherto maintained.

Philosophy is made to take a humbler place. Exact knowledge can be reached only by the methods of the sciences, but there is a range of speculative questions beyond the scope of the sciences. Theology appeals to revelation or tradition for answers to such questions, but the philosopher deals with them to the extent that they are accessible to human reason by itself. This is a point of view which Russell had already expressed with all possible clearness in his extremely entertaining but highly misleading work on the history of philosophy.

> All *definite* knowledge—so I should contend—belongs to science; all *dogma* as to what surpasses definite knowledge belongs to theology. But between theology and science there is a No Man's Land, exposed to attack from both sides; this No Man's Land is philosophy.[1]

Hence the first part of *Human Knowledge* is an account of the world of science, of those aspects of fact of which, in Russell's opinion, we have exact and definite knowledge.

The data at which philosophical analysis arrives are the same as before, and Russell maintains his denial of consciousness as a distinctive type of fact. "The distinction between 'seeing the sun' as a mental event, and the immediate object of my seeing, is now generally rejected as invalid, and in this view I concur."[2] Hence minds and material objects are interpreted as constructions out of

---

[1] *History of Western Philosophy*, London, 1946, p. 10.
[2] *Human Knowledge*, London, 1948, pp. 220–1.

sense-data and sensibilia in a way which is already familiar to the readers of the earlier Russell.

An important difference, however, is that what we suppose to be data are no longer regarded as unquestionable. "I think we should hold that the degree of credibility to be attached to a datum is sometimes a datum, and sometimes (perhaps always) falls short of certainty."[1] Philosophy, then, draws probable conclusions from probable data. Demonstrative inference is dismissed as leading only to tautologies. "Deduction has turned out to be much less powerful than was formerly supposed; it does not give new knowledge, except as to new forms of words for stating truths in some sense already known."[2] But probable inference is treated with more respect. Moreover probabilities can lend one another mutual support, so that a system built up on probabilities, while lacking the solidity of a system based on demonstrative inference, may nevertheless reach a degree of plausibility which is not to be despised.

> Given a number of propositions, each having a fairly high degree of intrinsic credibility, and given a system of inferences by virtue of which these various propositions increase each other's credibility, it may be possible in the end to arrive at a body of inter-connected propositions having, as a whole, a very high degree of credibility. Within this body, some are only inferred, but none are only premisses, for those which are premisses are also conclusions.[3]

It would seem that this recourse to the coherence theory of truth should lead Russell to retract some of the unkind things which he has from time to time uttered about Hegel.

Although this is, and is no doubt intended to be, a disarmingly modest philosophical programme, it is open to considerable criticism. For how can a datum in any sense of that term be merely probable? In dealing with probability

[1] Op. cit., p. 399.   [2] Op. cit., pp. 171–2.   [3] Op. cit., p. 413.

in Part V of *Human Knowledge* Russell wants to hold that, even when we estimate the probability of a proposition upon evidence, the degree of rational credibility of the proposition attaches to the proposition in itself. Thus he hopes to be able to recommend the notion of primitive propositions with different intrinsic degrees of credibility. But probability or credibility are not intrinsic characters of a proposition. A proposition must be true or false, however little we may be able to decide whether it be true or false. When we say that a proposition is probable, we are talking about the relation to it of the evidence available to us. Hence, if we judge a proposition to be merely probable, we may be sure that it is not a datum and have to look for the data on account of which we suppose it to be probable.

What Russell offers as empirical examples of uncertain data can be otherwise explained. The difficulty of distinguishing at times between perception and imagination is a difficulty of judging whether the source of an experience is an external stimulus or not; the experience itself quite certainly occurs. Uncertain memory equally presupposes a quite certain image; the uncertainty attaches to whether this indicates that we had a similar experience in the past. A dim awareness of logical connection in studying, for example, a mathematical proof is either the experience of expecting to see it in a moment or the memory of having just glimpsed it although we have lost it again, unless indeed it be a genuine present awareness, however lacking in stability and confidence, of the validity of the logical step in question. In any case we either see it or we do not see it.

What is new, therefore, in Russell's later conception of philosophy amounts to a confession that he cannot decide what really are data and so, also, what can legitimately be inferred from them. On the credit side, however, we must put his recognition that even the most tentative kind of philosophizing would be baseless unless we could presuppose some general principles about the world which are neither tautologies nor empirical facts. These bring back the traditional metaphysical concepts of substance and cause in a form intended to make them less disconcerting to contemporary empiricists. As Russell sums them up, they are:

I. The postulate of quasi-permanence [corresponding to the idea of substance].

II. The postulate of separable causal lines.

III. The postulate of spatio-temporal continuity in causal lines.

IV. The postulate of the common causal origin of similar structures ranged about a centre, or, more simply, the structural postulate.

V. The postulate of analogy [corresponding to the principle of induction]. [1]

Russell insists for the comfort of his friends that we need not assert these principles with more than probability and that they need not state more than what is usually the case. Nevertheless it will easily be seen that they constitute an embryonic metaphysic. Russell is to be congratulated both on the persistent vigour of thought which has led him to acknowledge so much at last and on the candour with which he admits the ultimate inadequacy of the pure empiricism which he gave so much of his life to uphold.

If Russell has thus become a reluctant convert to something like metaphysics, it is not to be supposed that he has converted his followers. The result of the comparative failure of his and Moore's empirical analyses has rather been a fatal impression that the appeal to experience inevitably leads back to the position of Hume. Recent British philosophers have tried various means of making themselves at home in a Humian world.

[1] Op. cit., p. 506. Words in square brackets are my own.

Chapter V

Wittgenstein and the Cult of Language

I

To TAKE a justly proportioned view of Wittgenstein is no easy task even since the posthumous publication of *Philosophical Investigations*, but it was harder still in the author's lifetime, and there is no cause for wonder that few had the courage to attempt it. As is well known, Wittgenstein himself, apart from a brief and rapidly diśavowed contribution to the joint meeting of the Aristotelian Society and Mind Association in 1929, printed nothing but the *Tractatus Logico-Philosophicus*, and that was as far back as 1922. The *Tractatus*, with its rapid staccato sentences like machine-gun fire, is not the easiest book in the world to interpret. When, in addition, it came to be known that the author was dissatisfied with his book but communicated his new suggestions only to a chosen few, the *profanum vulgus* of philosophers felt doubly disqualified from criticism. How could we discuss a system which we might well have misunderstood on points which the author might well have already recanted? Meanwhile, we had enough to do in getting our teeth into the *Tractatus*.

Since the appearance of *Philosophical Investigations* we are in a somewhat better position, although it still seems necessary to begin with the *Tractatus* in order to grasp the modifications and even contradictions of it contained in the later book. Presumably there is more to come, and no final picture of Wittgenstein is yet possible. Nevertheless it seems worth while for the outsider to begin to record the impression produced by those of his writings which are already accessible.

For we are constantly being told that there has been a revolution in philosophy, and the Lenin of this revolution was certainly Wittgenstein, even though the equivalent of Marx and Engels may be found in widely separated figures in the history of thought such as David Hume, Ernst Mach and Frege. And the Trotskys of this revolution may be domiciled at Oxford. Has there really been a philosophical revolution? If so, in what has it really consisted?

II

The suggestion that Wittgenstein has been responsible for a philosophical revolution provokes a comparison with the Cartesian approach which has dominated the main current of philosophy since the seventeenth century. To put a familiar matter briefly, Descartes attempted a systematic criticism of knowledge by exhibiting our ideas clearly and distinctly in their genetic order and dependence on one another. He found that he had to begin with the awareness of the self which is proclaimed in the *cogito*.

If Descartes was an innovator in attempting a systematic criticism of knowledge, he was very much of the tradition in the emphasis he laid on the self. At least since Socrates European philosophy had assigned to the thinking, feeling and willing self a privileged position in the centre of the philosophical picture. Descartes' successors do not seriously question his starting-point and order. Even Hume's impressions and ideas are, so to say, the *débris* of the traditional notion of the self.

In our own century Professor G. E. Moore's enterprise, as it appears from his published papers on perception, was still essentially of the Cartesian type, asking how a self aware of sense-data could transcend these data and reach a world of persons and things. The inconclusive nature of Moore's admirably meticulous researches might well suggest a final defeat of the Cartesian approach. It might seem that philosophers had to look for another approach if they were not always to be brought back to the place at which they had begun.

One reader of the *Tractatus* at least had the following three experiences in succession. The first was the fairly common one of not having the faintest idea of what it was about at all. The second, approximately half-way through, was the impression of a radically new approach to philosophy. The third, on reflection after reading the book, was a growing doubt whether the ghost of Descartes had really been, or could really be, exorcized.

The ideal of clearness and distinctness was of course maintained, but the novelty of the approach lay in the invitation to examine language without troubling about speakers and hearers, those intrusive selves which had held philosophers fast in the egocentric predicament and had prevented them from escaping into a wider world. The fact of language—and language is a fact—appears to offer the readiest escape from the egocentric predicament. Perhaps one's confidence may here be deceived. To utter or to write words does not ensure that there is anyone other than yourself to hear or to read them. Nevertheless, the common-sense recognition of language as the principal means of communication between human minds lends it a relatively assured status as a public fact in contrast with those scandalous private facts of sensing and thinking which have caused so many philosophical headaches.

That Wittgenstein was in earnest with the elimination of the self as usually understood became evident when he maintained that the soul or subject of awareness was a myth because "it is clear that *A believes P, A thinks P, A says P*, are of the form '*P* ' *says P*". (5. 542). In other words, the alleged relationship between subject and object of thought is really a relationship between the proposition as a linguistic fact, uttered or written, and the fact which it means or expresses.

The *Tractatus*, then, invites us to begin by contemplating propositions which purport to picture facts. On a more comprehensive view the world consists of facts, some of which are linguistic facts or propositions picturing other facts which are non-linguistic. That the simple pictorial theory of the proposition did not survive Wittgenstein's later self-criticism does not make it less interesting in estimating the influence of the *Tractatus*. For the meaningfulness of a proposition is then made dependent on its presenting the elements of fact in the structure which they possess in fact. The firm rejection of persistent data such as the self and its embodiment and of the data of analytic reflection such as the notions of metaphysics and ethics does not appear to leave any claimants to the title of empirical fact other than what Hume would have called impressions and ideas and more recent thinkers had described as sense-data.

We are confirmed in this suspicion when we read that "what solipsism *means* is quite correct, only it cannot be *said*, but it shows itself" (5.62) and that "solipsism strictly carried out coincides with pure realism" (5.64). It is not much of a concession to add that the correctness of solipsism cannot be said when in fact Wittgenstein has just said it. It would appear that to reduce the self to a locus of propositions makes it only more obviously impossible to regard any proposition as legitimately stating anything about what is other than the self. Both your world and your self are the sum total of the propositions which you entertain, and so they coincide.

While, then, the *Tractatus*, on analysis, seems to presuppose a Humian conception of what is empirical, its doctrine of necessity is still more obviously Humian. The world of fact is left as a field of utter contingency. "Any fact can either be the case or not be the case, and everything else remain the same" (1.21). This appears, in the context, to be a dogmatic assumption. Only in logic do we meet with the possible, the impossible and the necessary, and this is simply because "the propositions of logic are tautologies" (6.1).

Logic tells us nothing about the real world; it is concerned merely with the manipulation of symbols.

With these presuppositions a Humian doctrine of cause is inevitable. "Superstition is the belief in the causal nexus". (5.1361). The superstitious are commonly thought to be those who believe in a causal connection where no such connection subsists, as between spilling salt, or walking under a ladder, and incurring misfortune. But in the last resort no causal connection of any kind can be upheld. The concept of superstition should therefore be extended to cover belief in any kind of causal connection. Obviously, with Hume, we must admit that there are observed regularities in the correlation of types of fact, but observed regularity is just as contingent a fact as any other. We had no logical right to expect such regularities, and we have no logical right to expect that they will continue. That we have such expectations is, of course, another contingent fact.

Thus there is a complete difference of character between the field of logic and the field of the natural sciences. All that can strictly be said belongs to the sphere of the sciences, but such facts, including any regularities in their correlation, are utterly contingent and are accessible only to observation. Logic, dealing with formal relationships between propositions, does not really say anything; its deliverances are necessities because they are always tautologies.

Philosophy, which is evidently neither pure logic nor a natural science, has been commonly supposed to offer some general view of the universe on the basis of reflective analysis and inference. But on the doctrine of the *Tractatus* mere thinking cannot take us beyond the tautologies of logic and mathematics, and the real world is accessible only to the methods of the natural sciences. Hence philosophies, if they are metaphysical systems, must be nonsensical.

Nevertheless, if we have to surrender the positive function attributed to philosophy in the past, philosophy retains an important negative function. "The result of philosophy is not a number of 'philosophical propositions' but to make propositions clear" (4.112). It clarifies our thinking by making plain whether we are really saying anything and what it is precisely that we are saying; it purges language of the meaningless. In order to do this the philosopher has to draw the line between what can be said and what cannot be said, and consequently, in talking of what cannot be said, he must in a way talk nonsense; but a critical and elucidatory philosophy is useful nonsense, as contrasted with the useless nonsense of metaphysics, for it deflects us back from nonsense into sense. The final purpose of philosophy is to make itself superfluous by establishing us firmly on the right side of the barrier between sense and nonsense.

It is these aspects of the teaching of the *Tractatus* which lead to second thoughts about the novelty of its method of approach. Whatever may be said of Wittgenstein's formal starting-point, his philosophy seems to presuppose a Humian metaphysic. His propositions seem to turn out in the end to be as much the *débris* of a Cartesian self as were Hume's impressions and ideas. It does not appear that the logical positivists of yesterday were so mistaken as they are now sometimes said to have been in invoking the *Tractatus*.

Yet there are other aspects of the *Tractatus* to be taken into account. In the first place there is a suggested analysis of facts into things or objects in relation. What are these things or objects which "form the substance of the world" (2.021) and "are only differentiated from one another in that they are different" (2.0233)? They appear to be logical simples and to resemble Platonic ideas. We may recall by way of analogy the suggestion once made by Russell that genuine universals, such as must be admitted at least in the category of relation, were really identical in all their instances, and the way in which Whitehead speaks of the ingression of eternal objects into actual occasions. At any rate, it can be gathered from the *Tractatus* that these ultimate elements of fact are logically simple and do not by themselves exist or characterize the world; it is only as interrelated that they constitute the facts whose totality is the world. The reader of the *Tractatus* is left with a desire to hear more about these enigmatic elements of fact.

Secondly, there is the contrast between what can be said and what shows itself. This contrast appears in connection with the form of the proposition. For if a proposition pictures fact, the way in which it pictures fact cannot itself be pictured. "The picture, however, cannot represent its form of representation; it shows it forth" (2.172). But the form of the proposition is a picturing of the way in which things hang together, the structure of the real world itself. Hence it is not so surprising as it might seem that, in that well-known series of epigrams towards the end of the *Tractatus*, Wittgenstein identifies the inexpressible with the mystical. This is a sphere in which we can say nothing, not because the questions are unanswerable but because questions have vanished. "We feel that even if *all possible* scientific questions be answered, the problems of life have still not been touched at all. Of course there is then no question left, and just this is the answer" (6.52).

At this point we are tempted to turn Wittgenstein on his head and to represent him as holding that everything really worth saying is beyond the grasp of scientific thought. We might expect him to go on like Heidegger or Jaspers and to suggest to us how to become receptive to the self-revelation of *das Sein*. That, however, would be going far beyond the text if not, perhaps, beyond the man.

Yet the final impression left by the *Tractatus* is that Wittgenstein remained a speculative metaphysician in spite of himself and only by heroic efforts restrained himself from saying what on his logical principles cannot be said. If the bulk of the work could well be described as a philosophy to end all philosophies, there remain important hints that two sides of Wittgenstein's thinking are still at war. Nothing but perfect clearness can satisfy the Wittgenstein who defines the scope of language, and, paring away all that seems less than perfectly clear, he leaves us with a world of atomic facts which are combinations of logical simples and in which the sole concession to our habitual notion of mind is the admission that some of these facts are propositions which picture facts which are not propositions. It is a world in which there are no permanent substances with attributes and activities and no necessary correlations. Logic can tell us only how to replace one set of symbols by another with the same meaning, and philosophy is merely a way of making us talk sense by displaying nonsense for what it is. Yet, all the time, Wittgenstein was passionately convinced that behind this desiccated world of exact language was what could not be said but showed itself, and his overt scepticism was always on the point of becoming that very different and eventually quite positive thing, a cloud of unknowing.

III

If it was in this spirit that we read the *Tractatus*, it is easy to see why *Philosophical Investigations* should be a disappointment. For the points on which we hoped for further enlightenment are not there developed at all. It may well be, as has been suggested, that the main value of the work lies in incidental discussions of specific situations, but the work as a whole is dominated by a negative theme. If the *Tractatus* can be considered in Cartesian terms as an attempt to escape from the *cogito* and its implications, *Philosophical Investigations* represents an abdication of the ideal of distinctness. The quest for clearness, of course, remains.

The theme of the posthumous book can be found in the *Tractatus* in the sentence which runs: "In philosophy the question 'Why do we really use that word, that proposition?' constantly leads to valuable results" (6.211). This has now become the chief, and almost the only, type-question of philosophy, and the book is less a systematic account of the

73

varieties of linguistic usage than a polemic against the pretence of reducing these varieties to order. The rigid criterion of meaning contained in the picture theory of the proposition has given place to the opposite extreme of an infinite elasticity in the notion of meaning. The criterion of the proper use of language is now pragmatic. Does it succeed in the purpose for which it is intended? If so, there is nothing more which needs to be said about it, and the variety of purposes for which language may be used is inexhaustible.

The device of language-games, in which some aspect of linguistic usage is displayed in relative isolation, points the moral. There is no limit to the variety of possible language-games, and in actual speech and writing we are constantly playing different language-games with the same words. Games no doubt have their rules, but the rules of language-games are as flexible as those of croquet in *Alice in Wonderland*. "Is there not also the case where we play—and make up the rules as we go along? And there is even one where we alter them—as we go along?" (§ 83). The most that we can expect is a certain measure of consistency in the rules of our language-games and a certain family likeness between different language-games. By a family likeness is meant not a single similarity but the combinations of a group of repeatable characteristics taken any number at a time.

The important philosophical application of this pragmatic theory of language is that it is always senseless to ask what is *the* meaning of a word or *the* analysis of what it means. "When philosophers use a word—'knowledge', 'being', 'object', 'I', 'proposition', 'name'—and try to grasp the *essence* of the thing, one must always ask oneself: is the word ever actually used in this way in the language-game which is its original home?" (§ 116.) The function of the philosopher is, therefore, one of critical linguistic analysis in specific cases.

When we are able to use language without ambiguity or embarrassment, philosophy has nothing to say, for it would be a waste of time to analyse our meaning or to refurbish it in other terms. A broom may, if you like, be analysed into a brush and a stick, but it is usually more to the point to refer to it simply as a broom. When, however, our use of language seems to present us with riddles and paradoxes, it is the duty of the philosopher to show us that we are misunderstanding the language-game which we are trying to play. "It is not our aim to refine or complete the system of rules for the use of our words in unheard-of ways. For the clarity that we are aiming at is indeed *complete* clarity. But this simply means that the philosophical problems should *completely* disappear" (§ 133.) By another route, then, we have reached the conclusion of the *Tractatus* that the purpose of philosophy is to clear up linguistic muddles, and this time there do not seem to be the same hints of wider possibilities which might be developed.

It seems, therefore, that the negative side of Wittgenstein's thinking triumphed in the end. Having been disappointed in the hopes of absolute clearness and distinctness within a restricted field by means of a logically perfect language as adumbrated in the *Tractatus*, Wittgenstein fell back on a kind of clearness which does not connote distinctness. His view of necessity as belonging only to tautologies had always involved the denial of any deductive function to the philosopher. His later quest is for a kind of clearness which justifies itself pragmatically in specific cases and, since it does not involve systematic distinctness, is in effect a denial of the analytic function of philosophy in so far as this is an ontological or real analysis. What is left to the philosopher is a therapeutic criticism of language which leads to no clearness greater than that of ordinary language at its best.

Wittgenstein seemed unable to tolerate any mean between exact likeness and complete disparity, between the univocal and the equivocal. Where there was no exact likeness, there had to be a chaos irreducible to any kind of rational order. Rational order had, therefore, to be confined to the spheres of logic and of mathematics, where all think-ing could be univocal and all propositions tautologous. Empirical statements had eventually to be reduced to a hit-or-miss use of ordinary language, which had to prove in particular cases whether it was successfully used or not.

If Wittgenstein had been able to acknowledge the inexact similarity which is metaphysical analogy and had seen analogy as an indispensable instrument of thinking and a genuine source of rational order, his philosophy might have been very different. When he comes nearest to this, in his remarks on family likeness, we wonder that he could have been content to stop where he did. For all philosophy cries out that human thinking is not the finding of completely clear answers to completely clear questions within a restricted and self-contained field; it is the finding of answers which, good enough as far as they go, always raise larger questions within an indefinitely expanding field. Analogical thinking provides the elasticity with which the mind adapts itself to the widening perspectives of fact as far as it may. This, at any rate, is a valid implication of the Platonic theory of forms which are participated by fact in different manners and degrees. Wittgenstein would not, I venture to suspect, have denied that this shows itself; it is a pity that he felt himself inhibited from saying it. In happier circumstances he might have been expected, with his special talents and turn of mind, to make a striking contribution to the discussion of metaphysical analogy.

IV

As it is, we find Wittgenstein associated with an alleged philosophical revolution, a revolution which proceeds under the banner of linguistic analysis. To what extent is this really a revolution? And how has it affected philosophy for better or for worse?

No one is likely to question the importance of a philo-sophical criticism of language, both a criticism of ordinary language in its bearing on philosophical questions and a criticism of the language used by philosophers. Philosophy cannot but benefit by the elimination of questions which turn out to be merely verbal puzzles. Yet it is difficult to avoid a suspicion that in the recent past the patient has suffered from an overdose of linguistic therapeutics. Enthusiastic practitioners have advocated an extension of philosophical euthanasia which would amount to a massacre of the innocent, and their bedside manner has shown a sinister preference for killing over curing. A philosopher who, like Wittgenstein, continued to look forward to the complete disappearance of philosophical problems cannot be absolved of responsibility here.

Many who would describe themselves as linguistic analysts, of course, do not confine themselves to negative criticism but go on to discuss the customary problems of philosophy while giving them something of a new look. If it is not yet regarded as respectable to talk once again of the soul, one can say a good deal to the point by discussing the grammar of the word "soul". But this amiable subterfuge can scarcely be described as revolutionary.

In the end "linguistic analysis" seems itself to be a misleading expression. The object of a philosopher's criticism of language is to examine its adequacy as an expression of fact, and an analysis of fact must proceed *pari passu* with the criticism of language. Either we have to maintain that there are no philosophical problems but only unnecessary verbal complexities, and this is certainly a novelty though not one which seems likely to be upheld, or we must admit philosophical problems which are not merely linguistic.

It has been said that philosophers in the past subscribed to the fallacy of one word, one meaning, and thought that their task was to arrive at some single and privileged essence in each case. Plato is perhaps here in view, but any Platonic dialogue is a sufficient refutation. Plato was not in the least unaware of the curious twists and turns of meaning. What philosophers have tried to do with words is to pinpoint a meaning which they consider important, in order to go on to examine the analysis and implications of the type of fact thus isolated. No procedure could be more evidently legitimate, and, if a modern authority for it be required, Professor Moore has stated with great clearness and conciseness in §§ 6–8 of *Principia Ethica* what he supposes himself to be doing in examining the notion of good.

In reality the practice of contemporary British philosophers, whatever the form in which they cast their reflections, shows on the whole a return to a conception of philosophy wider than was fashionable in the recent past and closer to the practice of the traditional philosophers. As the old problems return, it is plain that we are still in the Cartesian epoch with the systematic criticism of knowledge in the forefront of interest. It is true, of course, that we shall have a better hope of solving our problems when we no longer confine our primary evidence to the disembodied awareness which is implied in the Cartesian *cogito* and in the discussions of those other pure contemplatives, the classical British empiricists, but acknowledge that immediate experience reveals an active embodied self in contact and communication with other persons and things. In the end there does not seem to have been a philosophical revolution but rather a period of regression followed by a renewed tendency to expansion.

Of Wittgenstein himself it may be that we shall have to say that—in this respect like Spinoza—he was a man of genius who turned out to contribute little to the development of philosophy. To say this may seem unjust to a fascination which is abundantly testified by those who heard him and is certainly not without effect on those who only read him. But this appears to be the fascination not of a philosophy but of the personality of a thinker who was at the same time violently critical and irresistibly speculative and who, in spite of all the prescriptions against philosophical embarrassment which he so liberally offered, could not abstain, in his own phrase, from bumping his head against philosophical problems. This unresolved duality is the reason why, if more of his manuscripts are published, we shall go on reading him in the hope that somewhere he gave away his speculative side more completely.

CHAPTER VI

Logical Positivism and Verification

I

LOGICAL positivism being a fashion of yesterday, philosophers are at present somewhat anxious to disown it and to diminish its importance. But it retains a real importance, both because it crystallized a number of previous tendencies in dogmatic form and because in undogmatic form it continues to make philosophers suspicious of affirmations which go beyond the limits it assigned to thinking. Whatever defects Professor Ayer may now discover in his early writings, he must reconcile himself to having the first edition of his *Language, Truth and Logic* regarded as the expression of a critical moment in the history of philosophy.

The new realism of Moore and Russell had apparently ended in reducing the contents of experience to sense-data alone. The concepts of common sense and of the sciences were logical or linguistic constructions out of sense-data. The Wittgenstein of the *Tractatus* seemed susceptible of an interpretation according to which elementary sentences recorded atomic experiences. The Viennese logicians, like Carnap and Schlick, basing themselves for their view of experience on Mach, a thinker who had influenced both Russell and Wittgenstein, were elaborating a logic of science in which momentary sense-experiences supplied the whole material of thought. British logical positivism was, in its inception, an equally dogmatic counterpart of the Viennese effort.

Since, as we have said, those who were once logical positivists are now inclined to disown their original dogmatic positions, it seems best to discuss those positions in themselves without reference to any particular presentation of them. The fundamental dogma was the principle of verification, the statement that the meaning of a proposition consisted in the way in which it could be verified. An obvious corollary was that an unverifiable proposition was meaningless. There are, of course, plenty of propositions which we are practically unable to verify but in respect of which we know what observations, if they could be made, would show them to be either true or false. Such propositions cannot be dismissed as meaningless. In its more plausible form the principle of verification made verifiability in principle, not verifiability in practice, the criterion of meaning.

Even so, it entailed the dogma that inference could not be fruitful and reveal new truth. For it is precisely in the case of an inferred proposition that meaning obviously differs from verification. When the truth of a proposition is known by immediate observation, its meaning is contained in the observation which verifies it, but, when a proposition is inferred, its meaning is contained in the premises only if the conclusion is a tautology.

In the vast majority of cases, no doubt, inference in matters of fact is less than certain, and a denial that inference could be both fruitful and certain would require some refutation. But the importance and validity of probable inference in matters of fact are too clear to need much argument. We are constantly, with greater or less confidence, making inferential judgments which go beyond appearances, and practical life would be altogether different from what it is if we were unable to do so. We infer from the appearance of the sky what kind of weather we are going to have, as we infer from the expression of a man's face what his attitude of mind is. Such inferences are hazardous, but they possess a genuine degree of probability, and the meaning of the conclusion is evidently different from the observations by which we support it.

Nevertheless, in the first enthusiasm of logical positivism, there were thought to be advantages in reducing the meaning of inferred propositions to the observations by which they were supported, for this abolished at a stroke a number of problems which had proved recalcitrant to the analysis of empirical philosophers. How, for example, do we know that other minds exist? If this is supposed to be always a matter of inference, does it depend on analogies of appearance or analogies of behaviour or both? Something may look very like a man and turn out to be a waxwork. If we could say that "This is a man" simply means that this exhibits to our observation the analogies of appearance and behaviour which lead us to make the judgment, we should have got rid of what seems to be an absurd theoretical doubt. We might then claim that the criterion of verification had brought us back to common sense.

Unfortunately this is a case in which common sense cannot have it both ways. If we want to rescue our commonsense inferences about matter of fact from the possibility of theoretical doubt, we can do so only by attributing to such judgments a kind of meaning which is far from being in accordance with common sense. For it is too clear that we do not *mean* by judgments such as "This is a man" simply the observations which lead us to make it. If we judge on reflection that these observations are insufficient to set the conclusion beyond the range of doubt, we have to put up with the fact that practical certainty is compatible with theoretical uncertainty. It may be, of course, that not all our knowledge of other minds is logically inferential, but that is a possibility to explore by reflection on experience.

The logical positivists, however, thought that they had got rid of a vast number of intractable philosophical problems. On the assumption that the data of the senses were the only possible objects of direct observation, a proposition had either to be given a meaning in terms of sense-data or to be dismissed as meaningless. What were described as metaphysical entities, supposed realities which could not be analysed in terms of sense-data, no longer merited discussion. There was no longer a question about whether the soul or God existed. It was not even necessary to prove that they did not exist, for to say either that they existed or that they did not exist was meaningless.

Ethical propositions had also to be fitted into this framework. To say that something is right or wrong is evidently not a record of sense-experience, but it is not easy to regard such sentences as meaningless. Recourse was therefore had to the non-indicative uses of language. It is a fact that we do not use language exclusively in order to make statements; we also, for example, give commands and express emotions. If we took a poem and tried to render its meaning in the form of bald statement, it might be that a quite long metrical composition would be reduced to little more than "Boy loves girl". What we have left out would be the emotive colouring which makes the real point of the poem. So it was maintained that in ethical discourse the sole statements were plain matters of fact such as "This is a lie", and the specifically ethical elements were expressions of feeling or exhortations or even commands but in no case stated anything. The practical conclusion was that we might have our personal moral preferences but that the ethical field was not amenable to rational discussion.

II

While the logical positivist thought that he could abolish metaphysics, he could not overlook the existence of logic and mathematics as sciences of demonstrative inference. If his general principle was to be upheld, he had to show that these sciences were concerned only with the interchangeability of symbols and arrived only at tautologies. Some symbolic formulations might well be more convenient than others, but there could not be a question of arriving at new truth by demonstrative inference.

The positivist treatment of logic and mathematics exploits the arbitrary element in the choice of symbols to mean this or that, and seeks to interpret the whole use of symbols as arbitrary. If we use inverted commas for the spoken or written symbol and italics for what it means, it is evident that "four" might have been chosen to mean *five* or *six* or anything else. But once we have chosen "four" to mean *four*, what we can legitimately say about it is no longer a matter of arbitrary choice but depends on its meaning. "Four multiplied by six makes twenty-four" is a formula which might have been assigned a quite different meaning from the meaning which it has in English, but that *four multiplied by six makes twenty-four* is a truth of fact which we must recognize and cannot alter. Arithmetic depends on characteristics of groups of similar things which we must accept with natural piety and which the mathematical philosopher tries to make explicit. If we are arbitrary not only in our choice of symbols but in what we do with them when we have assigned a meaning to them, we just simply get the sum wrong. It is no use trying to explain to our bank manager that we propose to give a positive meaning to a minus quantity and thus to convert a debit into a credit.

In the same way, the logic of inference depends on the real characteristics of the relation of entailment. That "if P entails Q and Q entails R, P entails R", is true because the relation of entailment really is transitive. That if "P entails Q", it does not follow that "Q entails P", is true because the relation of entailment is not symmetrical. All this must seem almost insultingly obvious to those who have not busied themselves with recent philosophy, but those who have done so will perceive the need of emphasizing the obvious in this field.

While, therefore, it is possible to construct arbitrary symbolic systems in any way we please, the logic and mathematics which we can usefully apply to the real world depend upon what the real world is like and have to respect the nature of relationships which obtain in fact. But we want to say not only that logic and mathematics state truths of fact but that logical and mathematical reasoning can be fruitful or non-tautological. This brings us back to the old controversy about the synthetic *a priori* proposition, and we must repeat that there is nothing in the nature of the relation of entailment to show that all entailments must be tautological.

In fact, moreover, when we are not tempted to suppose that all entailments must be tautological, we can easily recognize that there are plenty of logical and mathematical generalizations which are not tautological. "P entails R" is not part of the meaning of "P entails Q and Q entails R", although it necessarily follows from it. Whatever the status of Euclid's parallel axiom may be, it is certainly not a tautology, and it is legitimate to ask whether it is or is not true of actual space. But again, this is not a question of empirical observation; the question is whether we have an intuitive apprehension that it is necessarily true. In short, the generalizations of logic and mathematics purport to be the expression of necessary relations between propositions or between numbers or between spatial configurations; they are not exhausted by the assignment of meaning to symbols or by the elucidation of such meanings.

This being so, there is no reason in principle why there should not be a systematic metaphysic or ontology, and, if the positivist restriction of the contents of experience to sense-data is rejected, the application of logical and metaphysical principles to an adequate view of experience should enable us to recover a satisfactory speculative philosophy. The decline in dogmatic positivism might, then, lead us to expect a revival of a more vigorous kind of philosophizing. This has been verified to some extent. There is a wider range of discussion than was regarded as permissible in the recent past, but negative influences are still strong.

III

The current preoccupation with linguistic problems has two opposite effects. It is possible and even natural, when professing to discuss language, really to discuss what words mean, and it has become philosophically respectable to discuss the grammar of words which would have been dismissed a few years ago as metaphysical and meaningless. But it is also possible to take refuge from real problems in a discussion of the twists and turns of linguistic usage. A good deal of current philosophy tends to degenerate into a rather tiresomely protracted kind of lexicography.

If we ask why people should want to take refuge from real philosophical problems, the main answer seems to lie in a lack of confidence. Philosophers may no longer want to assert dogmatically that Hume was right, but they are far from prepared to assert that he was wrong. What has been abandoned as a negative dogma subsists as a formidable difficulty, and the easiest way to be unassailable continues to be to assert as little as possible.

It may sound like a sinister recommendation of gratuitous dogmatism to suggest that we may see something to be true without having obtained absolute clearness about it. Certainly no philosopher should be content with hasty generalizations, and absolute clearness remains the ideal quest of philosophy. For philosophy involves the criticism of the presuppositions of ordinary thinking, and that analysis and criticism of the foundations of thought is capable of unending development. But the despairing feeling that nothing is certain until it is absolutely clear is equally an abdication of philosophy as a human activity, for it would leave us with nothing to philosophize about. Ordinary thinking is a human activity which needs no further justification on its own level; here the later Wittgenstein is clearly right. Philosophical analysis and criticism aim at a greater clearness and a more luminous kind of certainty about the foundations of thinking; these can be reached in a human measure. Absolute clearness is the end to which we must be content to approximate. That future philosophers will ask questions we never asked and make answers we never guessed should not overwhelm us. To suppose that this invalidates what in our way we have managed to see with some degree of clearness is an unjustified emotional reaction and not a dispassionate intellectual judgment.

Philosophy can thus be conceived as a progressive method of reflection without its being supposed never to attain any assured results, and such results can be presented with some degree of confidence without our presuming that they can never be made clearer or more exact. To recapture this really human view of philosophy as a human activity is as much a matter of emotional equilibrium as of intellectual achievement. Perhaps is it emotional equilibrium rather than intellectual power that is most lacking in contemporary British philosophy.

How is this equilibrium to be regained? The view that there is a central tradition of European philosophy derived from the Greeks and maintained by the medieval thinkers must wait for the last chapters of this book. Meanwhile, in our contemporary world, the Continent offers two kinds of philosophical thinking which claim a wider scope than British empiricism. These are the metaphysics of the existentialists and the materialism of the Marxists. Their claims deserve examination.

Chapter VII

Existentialism and Metaphysics

I

THE very considerable differences among the various philosophers who are often classed together as representatives of the existentialist movement elicit sympathy for their protests against being thus united. It would no doubt be possible to distinguish existentialism, existential philosophy and the philosophy of existence. Nevertheless the popular voice is not altogether wrong. There is a discernible complex of ideas which are present in different proportions in all these thinkers.

What is meant by saying with them that existence is prior to essence? The contrast may be of the individual with the universal. Plato bequeathed to European philosophy a definite bias in favour of the universal. While Aristotle declared in reaction that the individual alone existed and was primarily real, he was far from working out the full consequences of this declaration. Like Aristotle, we all tend to be in a large measure Platonists even if it is in spite of ourselves. The existentialists might claim to be the first thinkers who consistently uphold the primacy of the individual.

From a different but cognate point of view the contrast may be of the active with the contemplative, the practical with the merely theoretical. The sense of selfhood is the acknowledgment of ourselves as agents, active existences making ourselves what we are to be and engaged in reciprocal striving with other selves and the physical world. Apart from the primary recognition of activity the sense of the real unitary self would disappear, as it does in Hume. The existentialists recall us to the reality of the self as agent.

It is consonant with such notions to press the rights of the instinctive as against the reflective. Reflection is too often merely critical and merely negative. In the name of critical reflection philosophers have at one time or another sought to deprive us of all the convictions that we need for practical living. The existentialists again seek to recall us to the instinctive affirmations which it is fatal to sacrifice to the pale abstractions of an excessively critical reason.

If all these tendencies were developed to their full extent, we might arrive at a complete irrationalism. Such a label might be attached after a superficial examination to the thought of Kierkegaard and, perhaps with greater justification, to the thought of Nietzsche. But we must consider against what kind of philosophy Kierkegaard, and even Nietzsche, was reacting. The critical system of Kant had given way to Hegel's absolute idealism, in which the individual was swallowed up by the universal, change and activity were rationalized in terms of ideal dialectic, and nothing bore any longer a resemblance to what it seemed to the common man. It is to a Hegelian, F. H. Bradley, that we owe the protest against thinking of reality as a ghostly ballet of bloodless categories, but it was precisely against Hegel's own ghostly ballet of bloodless categories that Kierkegaard made his protest. It is not surprising that he found himself bound to emphasize the primary and evident reality of the living, active individual self in contact with the world of other selves and things and aware of his personal responsibility before God.

Kierkegaard did not think of himself as a philosopher but as exposing the inadequacy of mere philosophy, and it is the paradox of contemporary existentialism that it is a mode of philosophizing based on a protest against philosophy. If Kierkegaard can be accused of irrationalism, it is because he did not face the strictly philosophical issues raised by his attack on Hegelianism. Had he done so, he would have found himself with Kant's criticism of metaphysics to overcome. The important contemporary existentialists are philosophers who, deriving inspiration from Kierkegaard, attempt to return to metaphysics but are impeded to a greater or less degree by Kantian presuppositions. Such, above all, are Heidegger and Jaspers.

The study of the attempts of Heidegger and Jaspers to overcome the obstacles presented by Kant is instructive and interesting. In contrast Sartre gives up hope too soon and is content to rest in his personal reactions to a world regarded as absurd. Gabriel Marcel, like Kierkegaard, is concerned with the psychological and moral conditions for reaching religious truth, and he is interesting in that way, but he is too securely insulated against the analytic difficulties of academic philosophy to make much contribution to philosophy as a science. The philosopher who appreciates the rigour of the game will concentrate his attention on Heidegger and Jaspers.

II

Heidegger reveals the historical source of his thought most clearly in his book on *Kant und das Problem der Metaphysik*. His effort is to show that Kant ought to have admitted the fundamental reality of time not simply as a form of sensibility but as the mode of existence of the real self. Heidegger is ready to accept from Kant that objects other than the self can be present to us only phenomenally. A creative mind could know the thing as it is in itself, for to a creative mind the thing is not a mere object (*Gegenstand*) but a product (*Entstand*). A finite and receptive mind, however, can know other things only in so far as it is affected by them, and an analysis of its knowledge will reveal both its subjective impressions and the forms under which these are objectified. The way in which things appear must always be conditioned by the kind of mind to which they appear.

So far Heidegger is entirely Kantian, and his attempt to rescue the awareness of the real self begins with Kant's own recognition that time characterizes our knowledge more uni-versally than space. Only some sensation has an outer or spatial aspect, but all sensation takes an inner or temporal form. Then Heidegger looks at that part of the first-edition version of the Deduction of the Categories which corresponds with the third stage in Vaihinger's analysis of the develop-ment of this confusing section of the *Critique*. This is the pas-sage in which the productive imagination is suggested to be the common root from which both sensibility and under-standing spring.

Kant, of course, abandoned this suggestion in the second edition of the *Critique*. He no longer tried to go back behind the duality of sensibility and understanding, and was content to describe the transcendental imagination as "an effect of the understanding on the sensibility". Heidegger regards this as a betrayal of genuine insight and pursues his own reflections on the basis of Kant's earlier thought.

The combination of sensibility and understanding is essen-tial to any finite mind, for any finite mind has to be both re-ceptive and objectifying and must be endowed with both forms of receptivity and forms of objectification. How must we think of human mind prior to actual occasions of sen-sation and thought? Its native forms of receptivity and ob-jectification then prefigure the way in which things will appear to it. What is this but to say that it is fundamentally the power of transcendental imagination?

But no sort of imagination has significance apart from time. Imagination in the ordinary sense, the reproductive imagination, looks backward; the transcendental imagina-tion looks forward and anticipates perception. Hence what Kant ought to have found by his critical analysis of human knowledge was a self which, as transcendental imagination, looks forward and, as looking forward, is essentially in time. Not only are phenomena presented in the framework of time but the real self is essentially temporal.

By this correction of Kant, Heidegger supplies himself with the critical basis for his meditations on the finite self in its brief passage through time between nothingness and death, such as we find them in *Sein und Zeit*. But, of course, it is only the awareness of the self which he thus rescues from being merely phenomenal. Our experience of other things is still involved in the Kantian predicament. So it is not surprising that Heidegger has never been able to produce the systematic ontology to which the published part of *Sein und Zeit* was to be the phenomenological introduction. He continues to lament the contingency of human existence without being able to arrive at an absolute.

For how is being itself to become unconcealed (*unverborgen*)? Any view of truth which looks at it as a correspondence between thought and fact seems to Heidegger to place an intermediary between the mind and real being and to involve a concealment and deformation of being in the process. Such a view of truth he regards as the bugbear of European philosophy since Plato. But how the mind is to achieve an unambiguous contact with being itself remains obscure. We are not creative but receptive minds, and our thinking cannot be exempt from subjectivity.

While Heidegger, then, has made a valiant effort to rescue the consciousness of the real active self from Kant's phenomenalism, his approach is throughout conditioned by Kant, and Kant's criticism continues to bar the way for him to a general metaphysic of being. Jaspers follows similar lines. Ordinary knowledge, the knowledge of objects, is necessarily infected with subjectivity, for an object is inconceivable except in relation to a subject. All scientific knowledge, including that knowledge of the self as an object which is psychology, must be interpreted in the Kantian manner. But what of our awareness of the subject as subject? As soon as we begin to reflect on the subject, we begin to turn it into an object, but there is a prior flash of realization in which we really catch ourselves as subjects, sources of existence and activity. Similarly we have flashes of insight into the subject of subjects, the absolute subject which is the source of limited centres of existence and activity, being itself. To describe such experiences we have only the language of objects, a language which is essentially inadequate, but we may hope by stretching the resources of that language to make others recognize the experiences which they have in common with ourselves and so in the only possible way to communicate what we cannot properly express.

Jaspers' doctrine of the philosophical use of language reminds us of the Wittgenstein of the *Tractatus*. For both thinkers philosophical statements are in a way nonsense and in a way revealing, though Wittgenstein places emphasis on *nonsense* and Jaspers on *revealing*. We need not be astonished if the stern positivist regards the existentialist as a philosopher who enjoys talking nonsense, while the existentialist looks on the positivist as a philosopher who refuses to talk philosophy at all because he is unable to talk it with the clearness of scientific language.

III

Anyone who is concerned to restore a more comprehensive scope to philosophy must sympathize with a good deal in the existentialist movement. Its principal achievement is to have vindicated the experience of a real active self. Classical empiricism, culminating in Hume, came to forget that we ever *did* anything. The stream of consciousness flowed placidly, or even turbidly, on, but there was no point in asking why it did so or what agency it revealed. But the experience of activity, of striving and resisting, is no less primitive than the so-called stream of consciousness, and profoundly modifies how we suppose the stream of consciousness to flow. The existentialists have recalled attention to this primitive experience.

Unfortunately they have not gone far in the direction of a general metaphysic, and the work of Heidegger shows why they have not. A philosopher of a different school might suggest that this is because they are still too afraid of Kant. Just as British philosophers are unduly chary of contradicting Hume, so the existentialists have been unduly chary of contradicting Kant. In one way or another they are still inhibited by Kantian presuppositions.

We may well ask, therefore, whether they are not partially responsible for their own difficulties. We must not fall into the mistake of supposing philosophy to be too easy, for an easy philosophy is a banal one, but we may legitimately inquire whether the scrutiny of experience and the construction of a metaphysic are as desperately difficult as the existentialists suppose them to be. It is only if we accept as much of Kant as Heidegger and Jaspers explicitly or implicitly do that we shall find ourselves as embarrassed as they are.

In this connection it is helpful to recall that what Martin Buber has to say about the I-Thou relationship brings home to us how unmistakably real is the experience not only of our own selves but of other persons. We must concede to Berkeley that it would be easier to doubt the existence of a world of independent material things than to doubt the existence of other persons. In the last resort, of course, a reflection on the implications of our consciousness of activity and resistance will not allow us to doubt either. Yet the consciousness of communication with other minds has a special obviousness of its own which prevents us from regarding our awareness of persons as being in any way compromised by the difficulties which philosophers have raised about the perception of material things.

In spite, however, of the limitations due to their Kantian inheritance the existentialists provide a useful reminder that an effort to recover the traditional scope of philosophy is still possible. Unfortunately the obstacles which seem greatest to the average contemporary British philosopher are not the Kantian presuppositions with which Heidegger and Jaspers feel themselves beset, and the tortured and obscure language which the existentialists use is another reason why they are not taken seriously enough in this country. It is true also that, especially in France, existentialism has become identified with an arbitrary individualism of thought and conduct which is of no service to serious philosophy. A full account of all that is called existentialism would have to take notice of these irrational aberrations. We have preferred to call attention to those aspects of the movement which, because they depend on a Kantian approach, cannot be acceptable to those who would criticize Kant more radically but which, since they aim at a wider conception of experience and a restoration of metaphysical thinking, are of interest to all who have similar aims.

CHAPTER VIII

The Philosophical Background of Marx and Engels

I

ALTHOUGH the writer on Chinese philosophy who looked up first China and then philosophy in the encyclopaedia, and proceeded to combine the information thus obtained, can hardly be said to have followed an adequate method, there is something to be said, when one is investigating dialectical materialism and its antecedents, for considering materialism and dialectics separately and then seeing what happened when they came together. Materialism is a recurrent mood of human thinking on the pre-philosophical as well as on the philosophical level. When our existentialist contemporaries point out that a denial of God is more than a failure to work out a metaphysical syllogism, they are uttering what is in one sense a truism but in another may be grossly misleading. For the atheist or agnostic is blind precisely to the necessity by which any instance of being entails as its ultimate source the fullness of being, and this is a metaphysical inference although it can be made inarticulately and needs in any case to be lived at the instinctive as well as elaborated at the logical level.

The mind which is, for whatever reason, thus meta-physically defective is confined in its search for explanation to factual correlations and temporal sequences within the world of experience. The world as a whole, instead of being seen as an overflow of infinite fullness, becomes merely a pattern of material fragments building themselves up into such systems as we call organisms, and collapsing again on the wheel of time. The spirit of materialism is essentially a contentment with proximate and partial explanations which leave the whole finally unexplained. The materialist cannot ask or answer the question why things should exist at all.

Yet materialism has its attractions. The specious humility which leaves ultimate questions aside as beyond a human answer often goes with a very real satisfaction in being the highest product of evolution and having acquired so large a measure of control over the material environment from which we came. There is a certain intoxication in rejecting anything higher than man and his works. This reproach is of course addressed to a dogmatic materialism and not to the puzzled agnosticism to which so many worthy people have been reduced by the modern climate of opinion.

That the modern climate of opinion is favourable to materialism is a fact for which science is sometimes blamed. It is not really the fault of science, for an increased understanding of material causes is both in itself a benefit and in no way an indication that more ultimate explanations are otiose. It is true, however, that an exclusive preoccupation with the departmental explanations of the sciences may make a man less ready to look farther, and the greater development of the physical as compared with the biological and psychological sciences has made it easier to acquire a materialist bias. That, nevertheless, is the fault not of the sciences but of some of the men who study them.

The growth of the sciences in modern times has inevitably had an influence on philosophy, but this has not usually been in the direction of a dogmatic materialism. Philosophers have concerned themselves with the status of the facts which scientists investigate and of the methods by which they investigate them, but they have on the whole been careful to preserve their more comprehensive vision. The case is different when philosophy is cultivated no longer for its own sake but simply in order to provide a general framework within which scientific discoveries can be exhibited and exploited. Then the tendency towards materialism is obvious, and we shall see that this is the case with Marx and Engels.

II

By a dialectic, in the present context, we mean an attempt to make history intelligible or to arrive at a philosophy of history. But philosophy of history can be understood in two ways. It may be an attempt to arrive at general laws of social change; and in that sense Plato and Aristotle were already contributing to the philosophy of history in their descriptions of the natural succession of political constitutions. Giambattista Vico at the beginning of the eighteenth century, who is usually regarded as the fountainhead of modern philosophy of history, was largely concerned with such general laws of social change, for his new science was about the common nature of nations and civilizations; he aimed at establishing the "principi di una scienza nuova d'intorno alla comune natura delle nazioni". Such an inquiry might equally well be said to belong to sociology or political theory in their dynamic or evolutionary aspect.

On the other hand, philosophy of history may be understood as an attempt to find meaning in history as a whole. In this sense it has no Hellenic parallel; the worlds of Plato and of Aristotle had neither beginning nor end and continued forever to manifest the same types of things. Even if the Stoics admitted a certain pattern of evolution, this was a pattern which was endlessly repeated in successive cycles. History as a whole acquired a meaning for the European mind only in terms of Jewish and Christian religious teaching. In the Christian centuries history was to be interpreted as a drama of creation, fall, redemption and judgment, and the first great effort to bring secular as well as biblical history under this conception was the *City of God* of St. Augustine. This, of course, was not so much a philosophy as a theology of history, and the Christian must in consistency say that only a theology of history can be adequate to the facts as they are in the concrete.

Although the perception of pattern in history as a whole was thus a Christian contribution to European thought, it survived among thinkers who rejected Christianity or whose Christianity was at least other than the Christianity of tradition. Hegel was not content simply to propose his dialectical formula as a general principle for the interpretation of change; he essayed to exhibit the whole of history as the progressive manifestation and self-realization of the Absolute Idea. It is easy to make fun, as Bertrand Russell most effectively does, with the details of the execution of Hegel's plan, but there remains something by no means unimpressive in the vast sweep of his effort of understanding.

It is a commonplace, but one which has to be repeated at this point, that the Jewish descent of Marx made him a Messianist although his Messianism was secularized. He was inspired by a vision of human history as a whole leading up to the stage of the classless society. But he was determined to be no mere visionary or Utopian socialist; he wanted a firm theoretical foundation for his practical activity. He found this in a combination of materialism with the Hegelian dialectic. So far we have glanced at materialism and at historical dialectic each for itself; now we must try to fit them together in the pattern which they formed in Marx's mind.

III

When Marx came to the university of Berlin in 1836, Hegel had already been dead for five years, but the philosophical teaching was still wholly Hegelian. Marx himself read Hegel with admiration and became for a time a convert to his system. But, as Engels has described in his work on *Feuerbach*, Hegel's followers were dividing into two camps. If greater emphasis is placed on the rationality of the actually real, Hegelianism becomes, as it was for Hegel himself, a philosophy of conservatism. The right-wing Hegelians, who venerated the existing order as the contemporary manifestation of the Absolute, were acceptable candidates for chairs in the German state universities.

If, however, greater emphasis is placed on the principle of unending change in Hegelianism, a revolutionary philosophy can be derived from it. The left-wing Hegelians, who took this line and with whom Marx consorted, were obviously not in the running for positions of academic emolument under the Prussian government. The expulsion of Bauer from the university of Berlin in 1841 marks the recognition of danger by the authorities and the moment when Marx himself could no longer entertain hopes of a peaceful professorial career.

The left-wing Hegelians, now driven into open political opposition, continued nevertheless to be idealists. Revolution was to come through ideas, and a revolution in ideas must come first. We are sometimes surprised by the vehemence with which Marx throughout his life continued to belabour such academic firebrands, but the amount of revolutionary idealism to which he had to listen during the early eighteen-forties seems to have left him in a state of permanent exacerbation with mere talk. He was too much of a realist not to see that revolutions made in the study would never go beyond it, and he evidently had less respect for the ineffective Utopian socialist than he had for the capitalist who at least knew how to pursue his own interest.

Then came Feuerbach with his materialism. In the Hegelian scheme the material world had been merely the alienation, the degenerate product, of the idea. Feuerbach reversed the order, recognizing the material world as primary and man with his ideas as its product. For Marx and Engels, who were already impatient with the futility of the revolutionary idealists, this came as a liberation of mind. "Enthusiasm was general; we all became Feuerbachians."[1]

---

[1] Engels, *Ludwig Feuerbach*, p. 28. Page references are to the editions of the Marxist-Leninist Library, London, Lawrence and Wishart.

But they did not remain Feuerbachians, for Feuerbach made no use of the Hegelian dialectic and operated with what Marx came to stigmatize as abstract and static conceptions of man and his environment. The dialectic was too valuable an instrument of revolutionary interpretation to be cast aside. The philosophy of revolution had to be a dialectical materialism.

IV

Marxist materialism begins reasonably enough as an epistemological realism. "We comprehended the concepts in our heads once more materialistically—as images of real things instead of regarding the real things as images of this or that stage of development of the absolute concept."[1] This is not a very refined expression of realism, for concepts are not images, and, if they were understood literally as representations, we should be faced with all the difficulties of representative idealism such as Descartes was forced into devious ways to overcome. We may, however, assume that Marx and Engels did not intend the metaphor to be pressed; they were trying to say that facts came first and were presupposed by an awareness of them. Orthodox Marxism has indeed always insisted on a commonsense realism in the question of perception, as we see from the rebuke administered by Lenin in his book on *Materialism and Empirio-Criticism* to those who turned aside in the direction of Mach's analysis of sense-experience. The similar impatience of Marxists with the sense-datum theories of twentieth-century British philosophers finds vigorous expression in Mr. Maurice Cornforth's *Science versus Idealism*.

If this were all that was meant by Marxist materialism, we should want to suggest that considerably more analysis and precision were required to make realism philosophically satisfactory, but we should have no ultimate quarrel with it. Nor should we want to quarrel with a proclamation such as the following. "It was resolved to comprehend the real

[1] Op. cit., p. 54.

world—nature and history—just as it presents itself to every-one who approaches it free from preconceived idealist fancies. It was decided relentlessly to sacrifice every idealist fancy which could not be brought into harmony with the facts conceived in their own and not in a fantastic connection. And materialism means nothing more than this."[1] This, after all, is much how we might have reacted to Hegel ourselves, and, if Marx on that account called us materialists, we might deprecate the name but admit the substance.

But Marx and Engels, of course, really make materialism mean a great deal more than this, and the worst of it is that they seem never to have explicitly acknowledged and tried to justify the logical jump by which they reach materialism as usually understood. What they now come to say is very different from an assertion of epistemological realism. "Nature exists independently of all philosophy. It is the foundation upon which we human beings, ourselves pro-ducts of nature, have grown up. Nothing exists outside nature and man, and the higher beings our religious fantasies have created are only the fantastic reflection of our own essence."[2] Marxism does not assert that mental events are really material, whatever that sentence might be taken to mean; it does not assert, to speak more precisely, that thinking, feeling and willing are simply identical with changes in the brain. Nor does it assert that mind has no influence on matter; on the contrary, it seeks to mobilize minds in hastening the course of revolutionary change. But it does hold that mind is wholly a product of matter and can have no existence apart from it. In that way it fully deserves the name of materialism.

It is not difficult to observe that a logical jump has been made. It is one thing to say that knowing presupposes being and that human knowledge presupposes material being, but another to say that all being is fundamentally material and that all knowing presupposes and is dependent upon matter. The former propositions, which are admitted

[1] Op. cit., p. 53.   [2] Op. cit., p. 28. Cf. p. 31.

by Aristotle and St. Thomas, do not entail the latter, which are a statement of materialism. But we should see wherein the intellectual temptation to materialism lies. When men, for whatever reason, are blind to the metaphysical acknowledgment by which the whole universe of time and change is apprehended as dependent upon a Being exempt not only from time and change but from any other limitation, a Being which is the absolute fullness of being, so that in the end only the greater can explain the less, they are confined to partial explanations in terms of temporal antecedents. In this type of explanation it is usually the less which helps to explain the greater; the oak tree is somehow the product of the acorn. On an evolutionary view of the history of the world it appears that things have gradually developed in the direction of greater complexity, first life emerging from inorganic matter and then mind from merely vegetable life. For a metaphysician such explanations are partial and incomplete, for a universe of time and change can never be self-explanatory, but, when such partial explanations come to be as comparatively fully charted as they have been through the modern progress of the sciences, there is a very considerable intellectual temptation to rest in them without going farther. Marx and his followers are by no means the only relevant instances.

For Marx, at any rate, it seemed that materialism was a natural corollary of any really hard-headed realism. He was content to rely upon the overwhelming advance of the sciences to make metaphysical explanations otiose. As far as religion was concerned, he did not make it his business to refute religious doctrine but sought to explain the varieties of human religion as reflections of social and economic structures. In any case, since religion was an opiate with which the oppressed classes consoled themselves in their prospects of the next world for the suffering which they underwent in this, it would die a natural death in the classless society which at last abolished the exploitation of man by man. This final consummation is the object of Marxist faith and hope and the creation of Marxist charity, and if these had not borne some affinity to Christian faith, hope and charity, Marxism would not have been as influential as it has been and is.

It is worth remembering that Nietzsche dismissed socialism and communism as being merely secularized forms of Christianity, offering the ordinary man an impossible future hope as religion had offered him an impossible eternal hope. In reality the ordinary man would always play the slavish role appropriate to him. The only remedy was to become à superman and to make sure that one was a master and not a slave. The paradox of our own day is that, where Marxism has been practically applied, Nietzsche's opinion seems to have been amply justified, whereas in the countries exempt from Marxist rule theoretical Marxism retains the quasi-religious appeal of humanitarianism. But perhaps this is a paradox inherent in any combination of theoretical materialism with moral idealism, when altruism, lacking respect for human personality, tends to degenerate into social engineering and the social engineers become a new privileged class.

v

In so far as Marxist materialism is dialectical it applies Hegel's scheme directly to the evolution of the material world. The gradual development of contradiction or antithesis, the sudden transition from quantitative to qualitative change and the eventual negation of the nega-tion when it is superseded in a higher synthesis all find their place with Marx as they did with Hegel. Indeed they deserve to do so, for Hegel's scheme, if not applied too rigidly and artificially, is a genuine contribution to the interpretation of history. On this side the Marxists are fully ready to acknow-ledge their debt to Hegel. Engels describes Hegel's chief merit as consisting in the "thought that the world is not to be comprehended as a complex of ready-made *things*, but as a complex of *processes*, in which the things apparently stable, no less than their mind-images in our heads, the concepts, go through an uninterrupted change of coming into being and passing away, in which, in spite of all seeming accidents and of all temporary retrogression, a progressive development asserts itself in the end". And, he goes on to say, "if investigation always proceeds from this standpoint, the demand for final solutions and eternal truths ceases once for all; one is always conscious of the necessary limitation of all acquired knowledge, of the fact that it is conditioned by the circumstances in which it was acquired".[1] In these passages, however, we see that Marx and Engels not only made use of Hegel's dialectical scheme but drew consequences from it about the inevitability of progress and the relativity of knowledge which need a great deal more scrutiny.

In their belief in the inevitability of progress Marx and Engels were typical products of the nineteenth century. In the mid-twentieth century there is no excuse for failing to observe that change can, even in the long run, be for the worse. The only ground for believing that, in the longest run, history is genuinely progressive is that it consists in the working out of a providential plan, and Marx had no such faith to justify his optimism. One likes Marx the better for being an unconscious Messianic prophet as well as the cool scientific investigator that he thought himself to be, but it is impossible to defend his consistency in this respect.

The Marxist doctrine of the relativity of knowledge is not quite so easy to pin down and criticize. On its philosophical side Marxism is evidently intended in large measure to be a philosophy to end all philosophies, for Engels goes so far as to say that "what still independently survives of all former philosophy is the science of thought and its laws—formal logic and dialectics. Everything else is merged in the positive science of Nature and history".[2] Feuerbach is attacked precisely because he tried to deal with human nature in the abstract and neglected the changing world in which men live and the changes which consequently occur

[1] Op. cit., pp. 54–5.　　　[2] Engels, *Anti-Dühring*, p. 32.

in human nature itself. "The cult of abstract man which formed the kernel of Feuerbach's new religion had to be replaced by the science of real men and of their historical development."[1]

When Engels descends to details and passes the departments of human knowledge in review, he admits some mitigation of his general principle of relativity. The permanent truths that he is willing to recognize are, nevertheless, apart from matters of historical fact, maxims of an elementary and trivial sort—"for example, that, generally speaking, man cannot live except by labour, that up to the present mankind for the most part has been divided into rulers and ruled, that Napoleon died on May 5th, 1821, and others of like kind."[2] It is perhaps more significant that, while Engels maintains that "all former moral theories are the product, in the last analysis, of the economic stage which society had reached at that particular epoch", the morality of consummated communism is described as "a really human morality which transcends class antagonisms and their legacies in thought".[3] It appears that there is an absolute morality to be reached, although we have not yet reached it.

The Marxist doctrine of the relativity of knowledge is not, therefore, very clear-cut. The perspective varies between a view of process as primary, so that not only things but ideas are subject to a dominating law of change and ideas are necessarily relative to the stage of history at which they are entertained, and the vision of a consummation in which humanity is freed from the shackles which have hitherto warped its life, its ideas and its behaviour, and attains the full measure of its potentialities. Such a vision presupposes, if not a Platonic idea of man, at least something like an Aristotelian entelechy, an end and perfection implied by human nature itself and giving a meaning and direction to the process which leads to it. It goes without saying that

---

[1] Engels, *Ludwig Feuerbach*, p. 51.   [2] Engels, *Anti-Dühring*, p. 104.
[3] Op. cit., p. 109.

Marxists do not feel at home with such conceptions, but it is difficult to see how they could logically avoid them.

A barrier against returning to this measure of what Marxists would call idealism is provided by their pragmatic theory of truth. No words of Marx are more famous than the aphorism: "The philosophers have only *interpreted* the world in various ways; the point, however, is to *change* it." [1] It would be a mistake to try to demolish this statement too easily by an appeal to Hellenic snobbery about the superiority of contemplation to action; the failure of so much academic theorizing to issue in relevant action is not a fit matter for complacency. But Marx plainly intends more than a just rebuke to philosophers who never leave their ivory towers, for he also says that "the question whether objective truth can be attributed to human thinking is not a question of theory but is a practical question. In practice man must prove the truth, i.e., the reality and power, the 'this-sidedness' of his thinking. The dispute over the reality or non-reality of thinking which is isolated from practice is a purely scholastic question". [2]

Here we must protest that truths should be applied in practice because they are seen to be true; they do not become true by being applied. To hold otherwise is to provide an excuse for a good deal of hasty thinking and even for a certain amount of plain lying. We begin to see how the tyranny of a party-line could be upheld, and there is no health in any group in which a party-line takes the place of honest thinking and individual integrity of mind. Pragmatism is not simply a mistaken theory; it cuts at the root of human dignity.

VI

We have tried to sketch the nature of dialectical materialism as it appears in the Marxist classics and especially in the writings of Engels, to whose clearer style Marx preferred

[1] *Eleventh Thesis against Feuerbach.*
[2] *Second Thesis against Feuerbach.*

to leave the exposition of philosophical questions. There is no doubt, however, that the ideas expounded by Engels are those of Marx, for Engels made up for a lack of originality in thought by being the perfect disciple. History shows no more harmonious and effective example of collaboration.

It is significant that the works of Engels which are of chief importance for Marxist philosophy are both polemical, the one being a criticism of Feuerbach and the other a criticism of Dühring. And the criticism, especially in the case of Dühring, frequently deserves the name of invective. Marxist philosophy was expounded piecemeal, and seems to have been thought out piecemeal, in the course of attacks on opponents. A practical and revolutionary purpose was always uppermost in the minds of Marx and Engels. Hence we should not be surprised by surviving ambiguities and other evidences of hasty construction.

In the sphere of general philosophy our main criticisms are of two jumps made by the Marxists without logical justification. The first is the jump from a quite sound if not very exactly formulated realism to a dogmatic materialism. The second is the jump from a very proper appreciation of the importance of change and history to an unwarranted denial of absolutes. When we have pointed out these defects we have given sufficient reason for not being Marxists.

Yet the fact remains that Marxism offers a general outlook which has aroused enough enthusiasm to make itself the dominating philosophy over a large part of the contemporary world. It is not an accident that it is congenial to many modern minds. The chief progress of modern thought has been in the physical sciences and in a knowledge of history. Marxism claims to be able to better the human condition by making use of the sciences in the direction of a line of progress discernible in history. For this purpose it presents an impressive unity of theory and practice. And intelligent criticism of Marxism will acknowledge what is positively sound in its foundations and worthy in its purpose while seeking to show that a negation of its negations will lead to a higher synthesis more capable of achieving that purpose and satisfying the needs of man.

The question is whether it is possible to get on dispassionate argumentative terms with the Marxists when the international situation puts Marxism and anti-Marxism more and more into the position of warring creeds. At any rate it is a sound principle not to lose one's temper but to remain as sweetly reasonable with opponents as one can. For argument is the only really innocuous, and indeed positively pleasant, form of cold war.

Part III

THE BASIS OF RECONSTRUCTION

Chapter IX

Philosophy and Common Sense

I

THAT men begin to worry about things when they have lost them or are in danger of losing them is a maxim not without application to philosophers. The question of the relation between philosophy and common sense has become important in modern times because its solution can no longer be taken for granted. There was no imperative need to raise the question in connection with the central tradition of ancient and medieval philosophy. Socrates assumed that, if he could get his young men to think sufficiently hard about their ordinary problems, they would begin to think philosophically, and that the end of the discussion would be not to abolish but to illuminate what they had already vaguely discerned. They would find out what they had really meant, not that they had meant nothing at all. Plato went on to exalt ideal contemplation above experience of this world of sense and change, but, although he put the latter in its place, it was a genuine place in the rational scheme of things in which he put it. Love of beautiful objects was to lead by a natural transition to the love of that essential beauty from which their beauty was derived. When Aristotle deserted his master, it was to stick more closely to the realities of ordinary experience, and it is a commonplace to describe Aristotelianism as systematized common sense. So, too, in the medieval tradition based on Plato and Aristotle, the philosopher aimed at knowing things *per altissimas causas*, but that was not to invalidate ordinary knowledge *per causas proximas*.

In modern times we have become accustomed to philosophical theories which turn ordinary experience upside down. We have been told at various times by the enlightened that when we think we are constructing the object which we know, and that when we act we have no reason to believe that it is more than a happy coincidence when what we intended comes to be. The unity of the person is itself an exploded superstition. Belief in the causal nexus is the very definition of superstition. Such views are now so familiar that they have lost their power to astonish, and it is only when we try to approach them with a fresh mind that we realize how astonishing they really are.

Meanwhile philosophy is expected to be paradoxical. The best hope for a new philosopher who wants to gain a hearing is to hit upon some as yet unasserted paradox and to discuss whether it is not after all necessary to take into account its claims to be true. A philosophy which maintains intact the general outline of our ordinary certainties is regarded, tacitly at any rate, as a somewhat grovelling kind of thinking, an example probably of wish-fulfilment or of the fear of facing unpleasant facts. After all—and this is at last a pertinent question—what is the use of philosophy, if it is to be no more than a laborious confirmation of what we think already? We expect the sciences to reveal fresh and exciting truths; why should we be shocked when we find that philosophy refuses to confine itself to the banal?

No doubt an unreflective acceptance of commonsense assumptions has done harm to philosophy in the past. This is strikingly evident, for example, in the problem of perception. Earlier philosophers were interested in the differences between normal and abnormal perception; they were impressed by such facts as that a sweet thing may seem bitter to a sick man, and so forth. But, although they recognized that things are not always what they seem, they were so convinced that things are generally more or less what they seem that they failed to realize what problems are involved in normal perception, what questions are raised by things seeming to us at all.

Yet, in the solution of such problems, can common sense be treated as cavalierly as it has often been treated in modern times? Could one, for example, ever be justified in concluding that things are never what they seem or that there are no real physical objects which appear? It is impossible for the mind to feel completely at ease with a philosophical system which entails a reversal of the judgments of common sense. There is a grave dissociation in the mind of a philosopher who thinks in one way on ordinary occasions and, in the manner of Pooh Bah, crosses the floor to think in an entirely contrary way when he philosophizes. Hume is perfectly conscious of this dissociation, but he tells us that we have to make the best of it.

Still, it would be foolish to accept too easily the existence of an absolute cleft between ordinary and philosophical thinking. It seems at least plausible to suppose that philosophy has some relevance to the rest of human life. Hence it is eminently necessary to inquire into the relation between philosophy and common sense if we want to be clear about the presuppositions of philosophy and the nature of the results which are to be expected from it. Such an inquiry has an important part to play in setting philosophy in its proper context.

II

The first requisite is to determine the precise meaning in which we are speaking of common sense. Sometimes the reference is to what is common to many as opposed to what is private to the individual, and then the appeal to common sense is equivalent to an appeal to common consent. Of course the common consent of mankind is an unnecessarily grandiloquent expression, because no one, however wide his contemporary information and his knowledge of history, is acquainted with the beliefs of more than a small number of the human race, and even among these it would be difficult to discover complete unanimity about any proposition. The appeal is really to the vast majority of individuals whose beliefs are known.

There is no doubt whatever that the beliefs of others, especially of the other members of the various social groups to which we belong, do have an immense influence in the formation of our own opinions, and that when we find that a view to which we incline conflicts with the beliefs of those about us, our confidence in its correctness is usually diminished. Nor, in general, would it be rational to try to exclude such influences. We do not claim personal infallibility and, before the event, others are just as likely to hit on the right answer as ourselves. Hence, when we find ourselves in opposition to the vast majority of men not only of our own time and place, in which special causes of error may prevail, but as far as our knowledge extends, there is a certain presumption that a mistake has crept somewhere into our mental processes.

This, however, has not much application to philosophical or scientific knowledge, because the majority of mankind do not consider propositions of this sort and have therefore no opinions about them. An appeal to the judgment of the majority on philosophical questions would be, as the argument from common sense has sometimes been said to be, an appeal from the expert to the ignorant. It must consequently be replaced by an appeal to the majority of those competent to judge, to the majority of the educated. It is chiefly in this form that Professor Stout interprets the appeal to common sense in philosophy.[1] Here the educated must be taken to include not only professional philosophers but also those of amateur status, those who, without being themselves original thinkers, have sufficient mental training to appreciate the philosophical thinking of others. The judgment of the amateur of philosophy has indeed a certain special virtue, because he is less likely to be led astray by the bias of the specialist whose vision is concentrated on his particular

[1] Cf. G. F. Stout, *Mind and Matter*, bk. i, ch. i, Cambridge, 1931.

aspect of the subject and on the special points which he has himself discerned in it. Hence it is always instructive to watch the impact of one's own pet theories on a mind of wide cultivation not committed to one's own particular department or method.

However, the judgment to be formed or to be tested after formation is always that of the individual thinker, and common sense receives its most important differentiation within the mind of the individual. Here common sense is distinguished from the more rarefied kinds of thought, from exact scientific and philosophical thinking. The problem of the relation between philosophy and common sense is concerned with the connection between philosophical thinking and those vaguer and more indefinite judgments with which we are nevertheless content for the greater part of our lives and especially for practical purposes. We must therefore consider some of the characteristics of this ordinary thinking which forms the mental background for the peculiar activities of the philosopher when he philosophizes.

III

This background includes a mass of experience preserved in memory, and not only of particular experience but of general categories applied to it. Antitheses like those of real and imaginary and of material and mental, as well as relations like that of cause and effect, belong to common sense before they enter the province of philosophy. On the plane of ordinary thinking, too, we make a great number of general judgments about the objects of experience, judgments to which we adhere with every variety of degree of assent, including, it is well to note, the highest degree possible. For although, if we are honest, we have to admit that our views, say, on politics and art are not beyond doubt, nothing could be greater than our commonsense certainties that, for instance, other human beings exist and there are material objects over against us, that is, independent of us.

We are fond of generalizing, but very few commonsense generalizations, if fully expressed, would even claim to be genuine universal propositions. The greater number belong to the type of assertion which says that something is mostly or usually or normally so. Mothers love their children, we say, but we do not feel that we have been refuted when we hear that the Society for the Prevention of Cruelty to Children has prosecuted a case of neglect, for commonsense rules are such as to admit of a few exceptions. The exception proves the rule because the impression of exceptionality which it arouses confirms the belief in the normal character of its contrary. Proverbs enshrine some of the wider generalizations of common sense, and the fact that they can sometimes be arranged in contradictory pairs shows, not that they are nonsense, but that they are not seriously intended as genuine universal propositions. If "out of sight, out of mind" and "absence makes the heart grow fonder" both have a certain validity, it is obvious that neither is completely universal.

What is more, commonsense generalizations are not philosophical propositions. It was the mistake of Reid and the Scottish school to attribute to common sense the first principles of logic and metaphysics. If this were true, philosophy would have nothing to do but to arrange and systematize what is known already, and it would be hard to believe that philosophy is either as important as we think it or as difficult as we know it to be. More clearly even than in Reid himself we find in Sir William Hamilton's dissertation "On the Philosophy of Common Sense", appended to his edition of Reid, that common sense is identified with the νοῦς which apprehends first principles according to Aristotle, the *intellectus primorum principiorum* of the scholastics.

But the degree of abstraction which belongs to logical and metaphysical propositions is simply not to be found on the level of commonsense thinking. No one but a philosopher thinks of talking about a principle of contradiction or a principle of causality. It is another thing to say that such

principles are implicit in commonsense judging and reasoning in the sense that, if they were not true, our ordinary
thinking would be invalid or meaningless. It remains
that they are not envisaged by common sense, and it requires a philosophical process not only to disentangle them
but also to discern how they are implicated in ordinary
thinking.

We have therefore to recognize that even the most certain
deliverances of common sense are lacking in precision of
form, and it often happens that commonsense beliefs are
inconsistent with one another. It is not unusual, for example,
to find a man who manages to believe both in the desira-
bility of the United Nations and in the natural right of his
own country to dominate the world. A more exact sort of
knowledge is needed to overcome this vagueness and inconsistency and, when the search for analytic clearness and
precision penetrates to the most central and most general
features of experience, the result is philosophy.

IV

Philosophical analysis has to be conducted, as far as
possible, dispassionately and without prejudice. But does
that mean that we have to throw over the whole of our
previously acquired body of experience and belief? Obviously not. If we did, we should have nothing left to think
about, and the mind would become, like the Bellman's map
in "The Hunting of the Snark", a perfect and absolute
blank. The same result would ensue if we tried to exclude
everything except what is absolutely clear and distinct, for
the attainment of perfect analytic clearness is the final aim
of philosophy, and it is evident that no knowledge possesses
it prior to the work of philosophical analysis.

Or should we, like Descartes, as he tried to keep himself
warm in Germany during that fateful winter of 1620, set
out to doubt as much as possible and content ourselves for
a foundation with what may happen to resist the effort?

Unfortunately there is always the danger that the effort may be too successful, and one may find that one has rejected things which can scarcely be done without and which there was really no sound reason for rejecting at all. Let us, however, be fair to Descartes. Philosophers have done their share in encumbering the world with verbiage, and the time does come when one longs to recover one's philosophical innocence and to try to see things straight from the beginning again. Perhaps this is all that Descartes was trying to do, but his words suggest more, and in fact he did more. In the stress of the moment he threw overboard a great deal of baggage which he found it exceedingly difficult to recover and which he really need not have thrown overboard in the first instance at all.

It is equally arbitrary to start with some highly specialized problem and to interpret everything else in the light of the solution given to it. Here Kant supplies the classical example, with the whole architecture of his system depending on a mistaken solution of the badly formulated problem of the synthetic *a priori* judgment. It is perfectly true that it is desirable to begin the work of analysis with the simplest possible situation, whether that be the apprehension of sense-data or something else, but it is suicidal to forget that such a situation is already abstract and merely an element in the total perceptual and cognitive field. The failure to take this into account is responsible for those philosophies which begin with sense-data and end with them too, though perhaps under a different name.

For there is no reason why any part of ordinary experience should be excluded when philosophical reflection begins. No part has antecedently any special privilege above the rest. Even the most vague of apprehensions and the most tentative of judgments demand to be taken into account, though of course with the quality and in the degree which belong to them. The total datum of philosophy is the whole of experience, and it is the whole of experience in its most general aspects which philosophy seeks first of all to analyse and make clear, then to correct, and perhaps also in its own way to extend. Philosophy therefore takes its point of departure from common sense and from the totality of the deliverances of common sense.

V

Although philosophical investigation begins from the level of common sense, that is no guarantee that many of its results will not prove surprising to those whose thinking has not hitherto transcended that level. It reveals unsuspected complexities in the apparently simple and supplies a needed corrective to our ordinary vagueness and cocksureness. It is liable to compromise the logical respectability of many cherished opinions. So the question arises, is there anything which it cannot compromise? Is there anything in the data of common sense which is not corrigible by philosophy? This is really the most important question about the relation between philosophy and common sense. If it is answered negatively, there is always the possibility that the final results of philosophical research may turn out to be at total variance with the deliverances of common sense, and there will be no help for it. If it is answered affirmatively, there will always remain a link between ordinary and philosophical thinking, and our total thinking will demand to be a unity.

The greater part of our ordinary thinking is certainly corrigible. In the details of life at any rate, we live by probabilities rather than certainties. I walk to the station to catch a train in spite of the possibility that, for all I know, there has been a lightning strike or an accident which is holding up the traffic on the line. We do not usually bother to advert to these possibilities which rob our expectations of certainty, but even on the level of common sense we should be ready, if we were asked, to admit their relevance. Nevertheless, in a settled state of society, we are able to make most of our arrangements with a view to probabilities of a high degree, and so their lack of complete certainty is not of practical importance.

Our more general views are usually also of a corrigible kind, and philosophy is able to assist in their correction. But it would be completely contrary to common sense itself to say that everything in common sense is corrigible. There are, above all, those data which, on the level of common sense, would be described as facts of experience, such as the existence of material objects and of other minds. The ordinary man would admit that he is at times liable to illusion, but he just simply knows that his whole experience is not illusion. Nor is it enough for the sophisticated philosopher to point out that these facts are not objects of immediate experience, for immediate experience is perhaps only of sense-data. The distinction between mediate and immediate experience is already a philosophical one; the ordinary man knows that these things are facts of experience, in his sense of the word, and are certainly facts, whatever their analysis may be.

All these things, whether facts of experience or not, are things which the ordinary man quite genuinely knows, and philosophy cannot possibly shake that knowledge, but would merely make itself ridiculous if it tried to do so. The irreformable data of common sense, it will be noted, are chiefly existential in character; commonsense generalizations, as we have already remarked, do not usually attain to complete universality and so, although valid in their degree, have a less definite standing and less bearing on philosophy. Logical and metaphysical principles are involved in the data of common sense only in the way that, if some principle were denied, it might follow that some experience or knowledge which we already genuinely possess would be impossible. The discovery of this relation is of course the work of philosophy itself.

It would be unjust to the irreformable data of common sense to describe them merely as instinctive beliefs. The Scottish School, while endeavouring to take out of common sense more than is in it, were nevertheless content to lower its pretensions in this way. Hamilton's argument, for example, is that the principles of common sense call for belief from the natural constitution of the mind, that consciousness is to be presumed trustworthy until proved mendacious, that no attempt to show that the data of consciousness are mutually contradictory has yet succeeded, and that consequently the original presumption in their favour is maintained. The contention that the structure of philosophy reposes on a foundation of instinctive beliefs often reappears, though usually nowadays with a more sceptical emphasis. It appears, for instance, where Lord Russell declares that "the opposition of instinct and reason is mainly illusory. Instinct, intuition or insight is what first leads to the beliefs which subsequent reason confirms or confutes; but the confirmation, where it is possible, consists, in the last analysis, of agreement with other beliefs no less instinctive."[1]

If it were indeed merely a question of instinctive belief, the sceptical emphasis would seem to be justified. The existence of an instinct to believe still leaves the question open, whether the instinct is to be trusted. If it were merely an instinct, there would be no possible answer, but the continuance of the unanswered question would entail a sceptical conclusion. However, the fundamental data of common sense are not things which it requires an instinct to believe. They are just simply there, presented to the mind as facts, and their evidence, on the level of common sense, is in themselves. No instinct, or even natural piety, only a refusal to close one's eyes to the facts, is needed for their acceptance. Moreover, the deliverances of common sense as a whole are a total datum to which philosophical analysis must be adequate. While correcting what is corrigible and accepting loyally what is irreformable, philosophy has as its principal function to provide an analytic interpretation of all the most general features of ordinary experience.

[1] *Our Knowledge of the External World*, London, 1926, p. 31.

VI

It follows from all this what value belongs in philosophy to the argument from common sense. Common sense is not a positive principle of philosophical construction. Philosophy deals with more precisely defined concepts and relations than are to be found on the level of ordinary thinking; it is the proper work of philosophy to reveal and discuss these. If, therefore, an appeal to common sense is a proper argument in support of some proposition, this proposition must itself belong to the level of common sense and not to the level of philosophy. For a genuine philosophical proposition an appeal to common sense is an inadequate support; the appeal must be to the more exact apprehension of relations which follows upon philosophical analysis.

But common sense has a very important function as a negative argument in philosophy. Since it is demanded of a philosophical analysis that it should provide an adequate interpretation of all the relevant features of ordinary experience, an analysis which fails to do so is known to be insufficient, and this state of affairs can sometimes be recognized on inspection. Further, an analysis which entails that no adequate interpretation of ordinary experience is possible is at once known to be false; this too can often be easily recognized. It is easy, for instance, to see that the Humian universe is not identical with the real world in which we live and that, on Hume's principles, it would be quite impossible that we should experience and know things which we do in fact experience and know. Hume himself acknowledged that his conclusions were in contradiction with the data of ordinary experience, but he does not seem to have realized that he refuted himself in doing so.

Common sense therefore enables us to know of a considerable number of philosophical propositions that they are false, but it does not tell us how they are false, and consequently, although it is a valid refutation, it is not precisely a philosophical refutation. A philosophical refutation can consist only in an alternative analysis which both justifies itself on the philosophical level and is adequate to the data of ordinary experience. This is the weakness of Reid's case against Hume—that, while quite properly pointing out that Hume's contentions do not make sense, he fails to provide any satisfactory alternative theory. The fact that a similar weakness has attended other attempts at philosophical reconstruction in modern times is presumably the explanation of the too facile way in which critical philosophers have allowed themselves to dispose of the claims of common sense.

But surely it is clear enough that philosophers ought to do justice both to the need of exact analysis and to the claims of common sense. The unity of thought, a harmony of ordinary with philosophical thinking, should not be an impossible ideal. Philosophy cannot be content with anything less than the completest possible analysis and the fullest possible logical rigour, but it will be none the worse if it continues to have meaning for the philosopher even when he is not philosophizing, and bears some visible relation to the practical life of the ordinary man.

CHAPTER X

The Enlargement of Empiricism

I

THE British empirical approach to philosophy has suffered three repulses. The first was when Hume, half rueful and half chuckling, decided that pure empiricism must land the thinker in a practically intolerable degree of scepticism, uncertain of anything save his present impressions and ideas. But empiricism plucked up heart again with Reid and the Scottish philosophers. Its second repulse was an almost silent one, when, after Hamilton, it slowly faded away. There can have been few more striking examples of a small mind succeeding in overshadowing a greater one than when Mill so superficially examined and so effectively condemned Sir William Hamilton's philosophy. At any rate, in the second half of the nineteenth century, those who were not content with a pseudo-scientific positivism found their comfort not in a more adequate empirical approach but in the prim paradoxes of a highly Anglicized Hegelianism. Once again, at the beginning of the present century, Professor Moore refuted idealism and gave new life to the painstaking analysis of ordinary experience. Once again the impulse seems to have died, and contemporary philosophers are satisfied with exploring language or at least are loth to leave their self-contained 'linguistic citadel and face the excessively fresh air of experienced fact. It would be inexcusably temerarious to throw doubt on the importance of semantics, but it may be permissible to hint that this is not the whole of philosophy. While one should go beyond empiricism rather than linger on this side of it, the revival of a genuinely empirical approach may well be a modest but necessary beginning.

One of the landmarks in the contemporary repulse of empiricism was surely Bertrand Russell's rejection of the existence of consciousness. This was, of course, as Russell declared, a repetition of James's negation, but it was something new in British empiricism. Nevertheless it appears in retrospect to have been not altogether unprepared. While the analysts of experience had been speaking freely enough of awareness as well as of the enigmatic objects of which we might be supposed to be immediately aware, all the limelight had been thrown on these objects, sense-data and images, and their possible combinations and elaborations. Awareness was a shadowy spectator, and it seemed that the play might go on equally well without it. Doubtless there is little point in acting a play without an audience, but it is equally true that a well-bred audience takes no part in the play, and in any case philosophers had given up the idealistic and anthropomorphic aim of finding a point in anything. Hence consciousness could disappear easily enough and leave the philosopher with the simplified task of interpreting all our notions as logical constructions out of sense-data and images. It was all very like Hume, but a Hume who took himself with deadly seriousness and suffered no recall to common sense by the clamorous necessities of practical life.

Needless to say, this highly sophisticated game with a limited selection of philosophical bricks could not engross attention for ever. Mind had to come back somehow. It came back through the analysis of meaning. Whatever may be the precise meaning of meaning, it is not simply a construction out of sense-data and images but something of a unique sort which supervenes upon them. A semantic universe of discourse had to be recognized along with the physical universe, however this latter might in the last resort be analysed. Although the first fine careless semantic rapture has perhaps passed, this is as far as many philosophers have attained up to the present. Whether they will suffer a disillusionment and emotional reaction which will turn them into existentialists on the Continental model is a speculation into which it would be gratuitous to enter. At present, at least, a great number of British philosophers trust themselves to speak of nothing but linguistic facts of meaning and physical facts of sensation and imagery.

What can be said about this development of thought and about its presuppositions? In the first place, let us admit that there are moments when the Humian and Russellian simplification enjoys a certain plausibility. We can put ourselves into a state of mind when we—active, substantial selves—somehow seem to disappear, and reality becomes an interminable and meaningless succession of incidents, in which the actors are not even things but the sensible shadows of things, and which is played at a speed which the slickest American film cannot rival. Yet, when we come back to real life again, it is evident that we have shut something off in reaching this curious state. The familiar example of meaning will illustrate what we have shut off. When we find that something means something else, we cannot possibly interpret the situation as being just simply a relationship between the meaningful and what it means. We must be aware of the meaningful in order to be aware of its meaning, and the relationship of meaning can occur only in a mind which envisages and correlates both its terms. We cannot dispense with a distinctive notion of awareness, but, in bringing it back, we must assign it a role which will prevent it from being so easily expelled again.

The suggestion which we are going to make traverses a common philosophical assumption. It has been pretty generally assumed that there is a fairly exact parallel between sensation and thought, sensation being an awareness of one kind of object and thought an awareness of another. In its commonest form this is an assertion that sensation is an awareness of particulars and thought of universals. We want to suggest here that sensation and thought are not awareness or knowing in any precisely similar sense at all. That there is an analogy between sensation and thought, on account of which it is reasonable to use of both a general term such as awareness or knowing, we should not be so foolish as to deny. But a merely analogical likeness is not the same as an intrinsically abstractible generic factor. We are concerned to show that, while the former holds between sensation and thought, the latter is not to be found. First, however, we must comment upon the historical origins of the common contrary assumption.

II

We must, of course, as nearly always, begin with Plato and recall his sharp distinction between the sensible perception of the world of becoming and the intellectual apprehension of the world of real being, which is the system of the Forms or Ideas. Aristotle is sometimes, and with some justice, accused of being a captious critic of Plato, but there are occasions when we may think that he was scarcely radical enough in his criticism. In the present connection, after all, he did little but bring the Forms down to earth and turn them into resemblances between particular things, which could be the foundation for universal concepts. This is by no means a negligible amendment, but it leaves intact the contrast between sensation as a knowledge of particular things and thought as a knowledge of something other than particulars, even if it be only the universals which are founded upon their resemblances. It may be that we can reproach Aristotle not only for being insufficiently Platonic in overlooking the metaphysical development so urgently suggested by the timeless necessity of universal concepts and universal truths, but also for being excessively Platonic in accepting an antithesis of sensation and thought very like that made by Plato himself.

It should be remarked, because it has some bearing upon the sequel, that Aristotle is guilty of no oversimplification in the problem of the perception of the external world. He does not by any means maintain, as he has sometimes been accused of maintaining, that sensation presents us at once and unquestionably with an awareness of the external material world. His general view of knowing as a reception of form without matter has often led his interpreters to suppose that he held the function of what are called the external senses to lie simply in perceiving qualities which external objects already actually possessed in themselves. But Aristotle is far too honest and exact a thinker to apply his general principles to facts of experience without a specific check. When he deals specifically with sensation, he makes quite clear that the result of his reflection is to conclude that the actuality of sensation and the actuality of sense-quality are simultaneous and one; just as the sense-faculty, prior to stimulation, is only potentially sensing, so the external object has in itself only the potentiality of the sense-quality which it is able to produce in the sentient subject. Aristotle is a realist in holding that awareness always presupposes its object, but he is quite capable of recognizing, as he did recognize, that sense-qualities belong ontologically to the sentient subject.

When we have grasped that this is indeed Aristotle's view of sensation, we ask ourselves with a new concern how he thought that we came to a knowledge of the external world. His doctrine on the question is both obscure and interesting. The question, in Aristotelian terms, is of the apprehension of the common sensibles, which are first enumerated as movement, rest, number, shape and magnitude.[1] Later Aristotle adds unity as opposed to number or multiplicity[2] and, more significantly, time.[3] In another passage rough and smooth, sharp and blunt, are also added,[4] but these are evidently reducible to varieties of shape. In discussing the common sensibles we have to avoid falling into the glaring contradiction of supposing that they are the objects of a special sense which could be called the common sense, and it would be inadequate to say that they are characters common to all kinds of sensation. Rather they are, with the exception of

---

[1] *De Anima*, ii, 5, 418a.
[2] *De Anima*, iii, 1, 425a.
[3] *De Memoria et Reminiscentia*, i, 450a.
[4] *De Sensu et Sensibili*, 4, 442b.

time, the fundamental characters of body and are apprehended by the sensibility as a whole, along with all kinds of
sensation but in a different way.

Aristotle says that the common sensibles are perceived
through *kinesis*.[1] Interpreters as eminent as St. Thomas
Aquinas and Sir David Ross have taken this to mean a
mental movement or change from potentiality to actuality.
Nevertheless there does not seem to be any reason in the context why Aristotle should make an explicit mention of this
accepted general principle, and in the previous phrase he has
just referred to *kinesis* as one of the common sensibles themselves. Hence it is probably more reasonable, with Theophrastus among the ancients and Beare among the moderns,
to interpret the passage as asserting that the awareness of all
the common sensibles begins with that one of them which is
local movement. Aristotle would be saying that it is through
movement that we become aware of our own bodies and of
other bodies in relation to them.

The apprehension of the common sensibles, however,
differs from that of the proper sensibles in another very
important respect, for, while the latter is more or less infallible, the former is constantly subject to error.[2] For instance, while the sun appears to the senses to be no more
than a foot in diameter, we discover that in reality it is bigger
than the earth. This is where the function of common sense
seems to run into that of *phantasia*. Aristotle gives us to understand that the apprehension of the common sensibles normally begins as an appearing, which is corrected and made
precise by a further application of mind. Of course this
theory is inadequate and full of difficulties; in particular,
the notion of an absolute appearing in which there is no
primary awareness of a real somewhat, which then appears
to be or to indicate something else, would, if Aristotle intended it, be unintelligible and unacceptable.

Yet it would be unfair and unhistorical to accuse him of a
phenomenalism which he never systematically contemplated.

[1] *De Anima*, iii, 1, 425a.   [2] *De Anima*, iii, 3, 428b.

His teaching about the common sensibles shows him, at any rate, to have had a fuller realization of the problems of perception than probably anyone else until modern times. Moreover, it points to a very considerable difference between the awareness of sensation and the awareness of body. The nearest thing to it in modern philosophy is to be found in the conception initiated by Reid of the natural concomitance of a subjective sensation with an objective perception.

These obscure hints, however, remained buried in Aristotle and were scarcely utilized by later Aristotelians. The general Aristotelian view saw sensation as an awareness of some of the qualities of external bodies, while thought was concerned with the abstraction of universal concepts and their combination in judgment and reasoning. An exception to this neat antithesis came rather from a consideration of the reflective knowledge of the self. Here was an awareness of a particular which was certainly intellectual and not a sensation. Although it presupposed sensation and occurred in connection with sensation, as also with abstract thinking, it could in no case be regarded as being itself a sensory awareness. St. Thomas Aquinas was quite clear that the intellectual principle had a properly intellectual knowledge of acts of thinking and willing and of itself in those acts.[1] In general, however, the intellect was regarded by Aristotelians almost exclusively as a faculty of conceptual analysis and not of the awareness of particulars.

III

Now consider what happened when epistemological considerations came to the forefront. Very little reflection is sufficient to show that in sensation an object is not only—to use the convenient scholastic word—intentionally or cognitively but also physically present to the sentient subject. Since sensation and perception had not so far been distinguished, it was natural to suppose that this immediate object of sensation was a representative idea, a picture of the external thing.

[1] *Summa Theologica*, I, qu. 87, arts. iii–iv.

As early as Peter Aureoli, who died in 1322, we find the doubt expressed whether God might not produce in our minds such pictures of an ostensible external world even if no external world existed. Thus one element in the Cartesian doubt was anticipated by three centuries.

After Descartes had given full currency to the doctrine of representative ideas, it took a century for the pseudo-problem to be unmasked. John Locke was still struggling with the really insuperable difficulties which it involved. It should have been a sufficient cause for suspicion that the ideas of the proper sensibles or secondary qualities turned out to represent nothing. Nevertheless, it was reserved for Berkeley to reject completely the doctrine of representative ideas, with his principle that "an idea can be like nothing but an idea, a colour or figure can be like nothing but another colour or figure".[1] Thus, while he still calls them ideas, Berkeley's ideas are entities in their own right, although existing in the mind which entertains them.

Here arises a new difficulty, with which Berkeley was not so successful. If sensation is still taken as the typical case of awareness, we begin to wonder—since it involves a physical unity of consciousness with its object—how we can ever be aware of anything outside ourselves. Berkeley's theory of the notions, as distinct from ideas, which we have of our own minds and of other minds is, of course, intended to overcome this difficulty and to salvage an objective world of minds, but the theory is so slight and undeveloped that it had little effect. Berkeley himself, moreover, as everyone knows, was unable to arrive at a notion of a material thing other than a system of ideas. The natural consequence was Hume's tenuous little universe of impressions and ideas chasing one another in accordance with the laws of association. No one, and least of all Hume himself, could take that seriously as the last word of philosophy, but the way out of the impasse was not easy to see. It was a judgment upon Hume when the enormous apparatus of Kant's three Critiques was constructed

[1] *Principles of Human Knowledge*, 8.

in order to expand the *Lebensraum* of philosophy again and to present us with a universe—dare we say it?—even less like the real world than that of Hume.

Yet, when the Kantian tidal wave subsided, the old difficulties recurred. It is only forty-four years since G. E. Moore published "The Refutation of Idealism", but the movement which he so bravely inaugurated seems to have had its day. Once again sensation was taken as the typical case of awareness, and once again no efforts have been adequate to avoid the nihilism of Hume. Families of sense-data, groups of sensa and sensibilia, have been combined in the most ingenious and delightful ways, but they still impenitently remain sense-data and sensibilia; they have not yielded us the real world. If we are not to be content to supplement them merely by a ghostly linguistic world, we should be prepared to consider some modifications of our notions of sensation and awareness.

IV

The fundamental point to which attention is asked is the difference between having a sensation and being aware of a sensation. All our terminology about awareness, it must be admitted, is ambiguous, and it is hoped that attention will be directed to the facts and not to a language which cannot help appearing ambiguous. No objection, then, is intended to a use of words according to which, when we have a sensation, we say that we are aware of something and conscious of something; it is suggested only that there is a distinctive sense of awareness in which it is not the same to have a sensation and to be aware of a sensation. In one way this is a semantic approach, since it is concerned to reveal ambiguities of language; in another way it is not altogether semantic, since the ambiguities of language are considered not as the primary objects of investigation but as snags to be avoided in dealing with facts.

The most compelling kind of sensation will provide the most difficult example for our thesis. Is it reasonable to say that we can have a pain without being aware of it? Not, evidently, in one quite natural sense of the phrase, for in that sense a pain of which we were unaware would not be a pain at all. When we are made unconscious by an anaesthetic, we become, as the origin of the word implies, incapable of sensation, at least to the extent required for the operation. But there is another sense in which we can have a pain without thinking about it. Nor does this mean merely having a pain without analysing it or without pitying ourselves for having it; it means having a pain without attending to it. This is, of course, extraordinarily difficult; any acute pain clamours for attention, and there are not many stoical enough to pay no attention to pain. Yet we do know what is meant by trying to divert our attention from pain and to think of something else, and we know that we can be at least partially successful in doing so. The sensible pain is just as much there as before, although we are not indulging ourselves in the intellectual pain of having a sensible pain. Thus we can conceive a limiting case in which we have succeeded in wholly diverting our intellectual attention from a pain although we are still having the pain. When babies cry, it may be presumed that this is the direct result of some sensible pain, not necessarily of any very acute character, but without intellectual endorse- ment or control.

Consider now the more favourable case when we seem to remember something which we have not previously noticed. We begin to notice the clock striking only when it is halfway through its strike, but then we remember that it has already been striking for some short time. Must we postulate that we have really given some minimum of attention to the earlier part of the strike? This does not appear to be necessary; we may have been completely immersed in some other ob- ject of attention. All that seems to be required is that we had in fact the relevant auditory sensations; we can now recall them and for the first time attend to them.

We conclude, therefore, on general grounds of introspec- tive analysis which we have briefly exemplified, that there is a distinction between having a sensation and being aware of it. The latter situation may be called one of reflective awareness, but it is really what primarily deserves the name of awareness. For, when we examine that of which we are aware when we are reflectively aware of a sensation, the sensation itself does not reveal any duality of awareness and object. The sensation is just an event which we cannot divide into subject and object; it is subjective, wholly subjective, in so far as it belongs to ourselves, and it is objective, wholly objective, in so far as it enjoys its own proper reality and is not an idea or perception of anything other than itself. This is obviously true when we reflect upon most kinds of sensation; it is less obviously true about sight, for we employ sight so readily and elaborately as our principal means of obtaining information about the external world, but we are able to see that it is none the less true of sight when we reflect upon the immediate visual object for its own sake.

We can see now, moreover, what it is that we are doing when we enter into Hume's or Russell's universe. We are trying to shut off the whole business of intellectual attention, or, rather, we are trying to leave intellectual attention out of account, for it requires a certain effort of intellectual concentration to do this. We are putting a ring round a self-contained universe of sense-data and images, leaving aside both our thinking about it and the ulterior significance which thought reads into it, and we are seeing whether we can construct anything like the real world by using only these materials. We see in the end that we cannot, or else our notion of the real world will be pretty impoverished.

A difficulty may be dealt with at once. We may wonder why, if sensation is really like this, we so naturally and readily use terms like "awareness" or "consciousness" of mere sensation and imagination. The reason is that sensations and their complementary images serve as indications of the state of the external world and of our own bodies. On the purely sensory level they are not apprehended as signs, for the apprehension of a sign as a sign belongs to thought, but they are not less behaviouristically efficacious as signs. It is not difficult to see how a sufficiently developed system of sensations serves as a reflection of the physical world, not by resembling it but by being correspondingly differentiated, and so stimulates appropriate behaviour in relation to the physical world upon a basis of instinctive reactions refined by experience. We have, after all, our own instinctive and acquired reactions to sensation which do not call for the intervention of thought or awareness in the full sense of the term. It is not difficult, therefore, to conceive in general what existence on the animal level must be, although we can scarcely take specifically into account the differences in the mode of sensation characteristic of various types of animals. The Humian and Russellian universes are perhaps, indeed, best interpreted as excursions into animal psychology.

v

Turning now to awareness in the full sense of the term, we appreciate that it is an absolutely distinctive and irreducible factor in the real world. There is no way of describing it except to disentangle it from what is not itself. We have seen that it is not in the least the same as having a sensation or entertaining an image. We can arrive at its elementary nature again from the other direction by distinguishing it from its own elaborations. Analysis, the apprehension of relations, the formation of universal concepts, reasoning— all presuppose and are differentiations of something elementary which is simply awareness and, in the first place, awareness of some real object. The primary awareness is an awareness that some particular thing exists.

A distinction is not uncommonly made between knowledge-of and knowledge-that. Knowledge-of, as distinct from knowledge-that, can only mean sensation and imagination. Hence we shall say that knowledge-of is not knowledge except in a remote and analogical sense. All real knowledge is knowledge-that; even our most primitive awareness is a knowledge that something exists and, consequently, it may be remarked, an invitation to indulge in metaphysics.

When we consider objectively what awareness means, we begin to wonder at the gratuitous tendency of those philosophers who are usually called empiricists to restrict its meaning to consciousness or awareness of something belonging to the self and, indeed, even more narrowly, to the consciousness of sensations and images. We do not begin to know anything about knowing until we understand that it is precisely the way in which we transcend our subjectivity. We are bound to go on being our limited selves, but the peculiar character and joy of knowing is that we can know what is not the self. *Obiectum intellectus est ens*, and, even if we have to begin with *ens sensibile*, we do not have to end with it, nor is this specific limitation characteristic of intellect except when united with a body.

The mistake of epistemological idealism, whether it holds that we are conversant only with ideas of things and never with things themselves, or that the sole realities that we can know are contents of consciousness (whatever that may be taken to mean), is dissipated by any clear reflection upon the notion of knowing. When we meditate upon what knowing is, we see at once that there is no reason at all why we should not have even direct and immediate knowledge of things other than ourselves. We are speaking of logically immediate knowledge. No doubt there is psychological mediacy when we know things other than ourselves; we can know them only, in so far as we are stimulated by them and attuned to them, but it does not follow that such knowledge must be logically mediate or discursive. We have to avoid not only the more fantastic error of solipsism, even of the merely methodological kind, but also the persistent prejudice that knowledge of the external world must be a matter of inference. There is no rational ground whatever for this assumption, and we are entitled to examine the facts dispassionately without regard to it.

The latent vice of what is usually known as empiricism is that it has implicitly regarded awareness as epiphenomenal. However it has defined the group of objects of which we can be aware, awareness itself has been no more than a ghostly accompaniment to the movements of these objects, keeping step with them as best it can in a silent and ghostly manner. In fact, however, we cannot understand true awareness, the awareness of thought, as anything but an original and irreducible energy in the universe of reality, not simply accompanying certain elements in it but laying hold of and assimilating the real as far as it may.

When we think of knowing, we must think of it, then, as existing in its own right. We must not think of ourselves merely as bodies in which there are certain curious phenomena of consciousness; we have to think of ourselves as beings which have, with equal primariness, both mental and bodily characters. Our mental side is largely conditioned by our bodily side, but so is our bodily side by our mental side. At any rate our mental side has its own characteristic energy by which it seeks to assimilate, in the manner proper to mind, not only the bodily self but the external physical world and the universe of reality which is wider than the physical world. If we have this realization of the nature of mind, we can progress from what has been called empiricism to an empiricism which deserves its name by doing justice to the whole of experience.

VI

On the basis of what has preceded we may attempt to indicate briefly and dogmatically what a genuinely empirical philosophy might be at the present day. It has to face squarely all those difficult questions about the analysis and evaluation of our commonsense beliefs which have been a preoccupation of philosophy since Descartes. If a philosopher tries to sidetrack these questions and take refuge in a purely abstract epistemology about the nature of the intellect and the nature of truth, he is not being empirical. But, in coping with the difficulties, he will avoid that autohypnosis with sensation which brought the first British philosophy of experience to a dead end with Hume and has had much the same effect upon the new empirical realism of the present century. When he looks to the past, he will find more inspiration in the wider horizons of Reid and, especially, of the mature Hamilton in his regrettably incomplete dissertations on Reid.

Realizing that there are other empirical data besides sensation, he will not make the mistake of supposing that he can evolve the consciousness of body out of an elaboration of mere sensations. Mere sensations, even of the visual and tactile kinds, are not three-dimensional, nor is it possible to construct the experience of volume by adding a third dimension to the two dimensions of visual sensation as it is in itself. It would be just as reasonable to think of constructing the experience of volume by putting together three time-dimensions. For the experience of volume is indeed an experience, and it is more precisely the experience of mass. Mass is a factor of reality which includes volume and is in that respect measurable in three dimensions, but it is presented in a unique and irreducible experience, and reality might contain other factors besides mass which were voluminous. The investigation of the consciousness of our own bodies must be distinct from the discussion of sensation.

Moreover, our consciousness is not simply of a body affected by sensations; it is a consciousness of a self possessing a body affected by sensations. The notion of activity is not to be found in the mere consciousness of body and sensation, nor can it be analysed into causality in the modern sense of a relation of determining temporal antecedents and determined temporal consequent. The source of the proper notion of activity or agency must be sought in the consciousness of the self which possesses bodily characteristics and is affected by sensation, and which is active in maintaining and developing its being, both bodily and mental.

The fully empirical philosopher will go on to examine how

we perceive the external world and other minds, without assuming in advance that such knowledge must be inferential. If there is adequate evidence that we sometimes have direct knowledge of external things and perhaps also of other minds, he will be ready to accept it. Nor will he refuse to look at the evidence for some direct knowledge of the past in memory.

With a proper understanding of the distinctive character of awareness he will not succumb to the residual Platonism which led Aristotle, when he converted the Forms into universals, to suppose that thought was no more than a faculty of analysis and abstraction. He will be ready to make a necessary modification of customary assumptions, which have been accepted much more widely than the Platonic and Aristotelian systems with which they originated, by putting the dividing-line between the purely sensory and the intellectual one stage further back, seeing analysis and abstraction, together with reasoning, as differentiations and developments of a primitive awareness of fact which is also the beginning of thought. It is the power of reflective awareness, which is awareness as a distinctive act, that is the fundamental character of thinking.

When he has penetrated so far, he will see very clearly that he cannot be a true empiricist without becoming a metaphysician. He has to find out what the analysis of the situation is when he is aware that something exists or that a subject possesses qualities and activities. The problem of being and the problem of substance and attribute arise as directly out of our ordinary experience as they are clearly enshrined in the structure of our ordinary language.

This is the kind of philosophy for which we may hope. Modern philosophy has lingered so long in its perplexities about the logical value of commonsense beliefs that the preoccupations of older philosophers have come to seem meaningless to many and are by some roundly declared to be meaningless. A merely antiquarian revival of the old which did not try to answer later difficulties would soon be returned to the museum from which it came. What we need is an empiricism which does justice to the whole of experience, an empirical approach to metaphysics and a consequent renewal of metaphysical thinking upon more completely explored epistemological foundations.

CHAPTER XI

The Possibility of Metaphysics

I

W E should try to make clearer the principles of method upon which the possibility of metaphysics depends. In the first place, ontological analysis must be possible. This is evidently different, for example, from the detailed description of the concrete parts of a concrete whole like an organism or a molecule. It is, so to say, an analysis in depth proceeding in the direction of greater abstraction and revealing, as a consideration of analogy will show more exactly, the fundamental variables which take this or that specific form and are instantiated in this or that way.

Among contemporary philosophers G. E. Moore has both practised and briefly stated the principle of this kind of analysis when dealing with the notion of good. One of the few recent thinkers to try to deal with the nature of metaphysical analysis at length was L. Susan Stebbing.[1] Some of her opening sentences express well what is intended.

Metaphysics is a systematic study concerned to show what is the structure of the facts in the world to which reference is made, with varying degrees of indirectness, whenever a true statement is made. . . . To know precisely what a given fact is is to know both the elements that make up the fact and the mode of their combination. In other words, it is to know the structure of the fact. Hence, the aim of metaphysics is to reveal the structure of that to which reference is made in true statements.

[1] L. S. Stebbing, "The Method of Analysis in Metaphysics", in *Proceedings of the Aristotelian Society*, 1932–3, pp. 65–94.

She indicates the fundamental presupposition of metaphysical analysis in the statement that "directional analysis is possible". Directional analysis is then said, under the influence of the Wittgenstein of the *Tractatus*, to be a reduction to basic facts. This, as in the *Tractatus*, is a somewhat ambiguous maxim, for a basic fact sounds rather more concrete than the constituents of a metaphysical analysis can be. If we are really to avoid the retractation of the later Wittgenstein, we must think of metaphysical analysis as being a description of the more specific in more general terms.

Thus metaphysical analysis corresponds with what logicians have discussed under the heading of real definition. In nominal definition we are concerned either with what we intend to mean by a word or with what people usually mean by it. The word is assigned an intension or set of intensions either arbitrarily or in accordance with common usage. Real definition supposes a more or less determinate extension of particulars to which we are already accustomed to refer by a common name, and we ask in what the unity of the class consists. We must not, of course, assume that a single distinguishing character can be found. It may be that there is a constellation of characters, the presence of all or even some of which impels us to use the common name. Moreover, when our analysis is complete, we must be ready to correct, if necessary, the limits of the extension to which the name applies. But, if we avoid the two snags of supposing that every word has a single clear meaning and supposing that common usage is an infallible guide to its application, the process of real definition is a legitimate and indeed essential way of making our notions precise. It is another name for metaphysical analysis.

In his book on *Definition* Mr. Richard Robinson is so appalled by the confusions involved in the discussion of real definition that he is inclined to dissuade us from using the term. In fact, however, he describes the process of metaphysical analysis very clearly, and agrees that "it is precisely the thing that the phrase 'real definition' has most of all been used to mean in the past".[1] His excellent book can well be read as a pointer to the most appropriate use of the term.

II

Kant's account of the analytic proposition shows him also as being well aware of the function of conceptual analysis. An analytic proposition is in some sense a tautology, but there are at least two sorts of tautology. The trivial sort like *"all green grass is green"*, merely asserts in the predicate a character which is already explicit in the subject. But a tautology is not trivial if the predicate brings out a character which has not yet been distinctly conceived, although it is really an element in the subject. Kant describes such a character as being contained in latent form—*versteckterweise*—and already, although confusedly, thought of—*schon (obgleich verworren) gedacht*—in the subject. The analytic proposition making it explicit is obtained by a conceptual dismemberment—*Zergliederung*—and is a purely explanatory proposition—*Erläuterungsurteil*.

If, however, there is to be a possibility of fruitful inference, we must also be able to affirm the kind of proposition in which the predicate extends beyond the meaning of the subject—*Erweiterungsurteil*. This is the synthetic proposition in the Kantian sense. When we acknowledge that no empirical generalization can be validated even with probability without recourse to some non-empirical principle, we can state more precisely that fruitful inference presupposes the truth of some synthetic *a priori* propositions in the Kantian sense. In any case, metaphysics is not an empirical science. Hence, if inference is to have any place in metaphysics, we must know some synthetic *a priori* propositions. The possibility of ontological analysis having been our first point, the knowledge of some synthetic *a priori* propositions understood as real insights and not as mental constructions,

[1] *Definition*, Oxford, 1950, p. 177.

will be our second requisite for the construction of a systematic philosophy.

Here we agree with Sir David Ross that

> . . . there is no more mystery about the knowledge of synthetic than about the knowledge of analytic propositions. Given the possibility of the unique thing called knowledge, then if there are necessary synthetic connexions between different elements in reality, there is no more reason why these should not be known than why the correct analysis of wholes into their elements should not be known.[1]

It will make the situation clearer to express it in the terminology of entailment and to add that not all synthetic *a priori* propositions are full entailments. Some are probabilifications of greater or less force. The synthetic *a priori* propositions that we know may then be divided into four types according as implicans and implicate are parts of a single concrete whole or are concretely distinct, and as implicans is ontologically prior or posterior to implicate.

When implicans and implicate belong to a single concrete whole and implicans is ontologically posterior to implicate, we have the relation of the intrinsically conditioned to its intrinsic condition. An example of this is the proposition that, "if anything is coloured, it is extended". A coloured extension is a concrete whole, but colour is abstractly distinct from extension and presupposes it. We just see that this is the case.

When implicans and implicate belong to a single concrete whole but implicans is ontologically prior to implicate, we have a relation of ground to consequent. Such is the relation of "being a triangle" to "having its angles equal to two right angles". Geometry largely consists in working out such implications of the fundamental characters of spatial configurations.

[1] Sir David Ross, *Kant's Ethical Theory*, Oxford, 1954, p. 42.

When implicans and implicate are concretely distinct, and implicans is ontologically posterior to implicate, we have another relation of conditioned to condition, which may be called the relation of extrinsic conditioning. That "choice presupposes deliberation" is an example, for deliberation and choice are distinct acts, but there could not be a choice unless the alternatives had previously been presented to the mind and weighed up by it.

When implicans and implicate are concretely distinct but implicans is ontologically prior to implicate, we have the familiar relation of cause and effect about which Hume started all the difficulty. It is in this field that we most need to be reminded that what we commonly observe are probabilifications rather than entailments, but the recognition of immediately intelligible causal probabilifications is surely a fact of experience. We just see that certain types of occurrence tend to make us depressed as certain others tend to make us elated. To suppose that apart from repeated empirical observation we should not know that the achievement of a purpose tends to cause joy would be an absurdity. On the contrary, whenever we find a man who has achieved an ambition and is not exhilarated by it, and however often we come across such a case, we always find it unintelligible. It is only when we discover the latent counteragent which inhibits the natural result of success that the situation becomes intelligible.

A scrutiny of experience, therefore, reveals that a recognition of synthetic *a priori* connections pervades our thinking. They will be regarded as mysterious only if it is supposed that the elements of fact are like hard atoms floating in space. On the contrary, however, just as the concrete world is given to us as a collection of things related in space and time, so our conceptual world reveals factors which are essentially in intelligible connection and of themselves point to one another. The intelligible relationships of our notions are the basis of inference.

III

A third presupposition of metaphysics is the power of analogical thinking. Without it we should be incapable of conceiving anything except what is altogether like the objects of experience or of inferring anything except instances of completely determinate general rules. For analogy is precisely the power of relatively indeterminate concepts to have genuinely new applications. Their novelty of application must, of course, be accompanied by a measure of ignorance about how exactly they apply in new cases, for we can know with complete exactness only what is exactly like the objects of immediate experience.

A traveller's description of Arabia cannot have for one who has not been there the concreteness which it revives for one who knows the country. The concepts in terms of which it is conveyed can have meaning only in so far as the hearer or reader is acquainted with something like them. But a good description conveys a significant unlikeness as well as a likeness to the recipient's experience. A multiplication and mutual modification of analogies can to some extent, although never completely, make up for the absence of immediate acquaintance.

Metaphysical concepts centre in the notion of being, and metaphysics claims to be able to say something of all being. This is because the notion of being, while derived from the objects of our experience, is evidently applicable beyond them. Otherwise we could not have a notion of nothing which is really a notion of nothing and not simply of what is other than the objects of experience. It is because we have this analogous but all-embracing notion of being that we can talk significantly, although with utter inadequacy, of absolute being or God.

An understanding not only of metaphysics but also of aesthetics must be based on an appreciation of analogy. For aesthetic experience depends on significant analogies between the realm of sense and imagination and the realm of the intelligible. But, while the ramifications of analogy do not concern us here, the importance of analogy for any systematic philosophy must be emphasized. The defects of the common sort of empirical philosophy are no doubt partly due to the assumption that words are counters with fixed and determinate meanings and that thought consists in nothing else but the manipulation and combination of atomic and inelastic concepts. A consequence of this is the view that we can have no knowledge whose validity extends beyond the spatio-temporal world of experience.

IV

Fourthly, we must try to bring out the difference between logic and metaphysics. For the contemporary philosopher often seems to suppose that he is dealing with the questions asked by metaphysicians when he is really considering the logical counterparts of these questions. The question, for example, which is traditionally intended in the discussion of the identity of indiscernibles is a question about what things have to be in order to be distinct. This is not the same as the question how we are able to distinguish this from that. The latter is a logical question, and it might well be in a specific case unanswerable, although we should still be able to indicate ontological conditions under which two logically indistinguishable things were really distinct.

In general, the logician is concerned with the realm of concepts as such. His concepts will be instantiated in fact or not, and his propositions will be true in fact or not, but his business is rather with the relations of concepts and of propositions. Hence the pure logician, as is very evident in recent and contemporary logic, fights shy of the notion of existence. This is all right as long as he is being a pure logician, but the philosopher is not only a logician.

For the metaphysician the notion of existence is crucial. By the existential judgment he passes from the sphere of logic to that of reality, and in the ontological sphere the notion of the existence of conceptual contents expands into the notion of being as the fundamental variable which is the whole positivity of things and which is differentiated by the limitations under which it is manifested. Logical distinctions can be indefinitely multiplied. Logically we distinguish a thing from its relations and we can even think of the relation of a thing to some other relation of it and so on. Such distinctions, as Bradley pointed out, cannot be distinctions in reality, but to speak of them as being merely distinctions in appearance is misleading in·so far as it suggests that they are illusory. They are legitimate distinctions in the sphere of logic.

The metaphysician, on the other hand, is interested in real distinctions, and the question whether there is a real distinction is the question whether a difference in fullness of being is involved. Here it is obvious, for example, that the likeness of two peas adds nothing to the being of the peas. To be a pea and to be like another pea are logically distinct aspects of the single real being of the pea. Equally, the attribution to the pea of the relation of being like another pea is another logical relation with as little claim to add anything to the being of the pea.

These are comparatively trivial illustrations of the difference of function and point of view between the logician and the metaphysician. It is unfortunately true that this difference is not well understood by many contemporary philosophers. That is one reason for the absence of metaphysics from the contemporary philosophical scene. In addition to recovering a satisfactory view of the contents of experience we need to relearn how to think in terms of being and to think analogically in order to appreciate the force of conceptual analysis and the way in which knowledge can be extended by inference beyond immediate experience.

Chapter XII

Is There a Perennial Philosophy?

I

THE scandal of philosophy is the disagreement of philosophers. Among the radical oppositions, amounting sometimes to an incapacity of philosophers of different schools to understand one another's language, the neophyte is apt to be discouraged from adopting any one of the conflicting systems or from adding yet another of his own. While the sciences go steadily marching on, philosophers are still hotly debating the questions which agitated the more cultivated of Athenian citizens over two millennia ago. All that they seem to have done is to multiply the subjects of contradiction.

We need not think that this is wholly a contemporary embarrassment. In the twelfth century John of Salisbury, revisiting the scenes of his youthful studies at Paris, found his old companions still debating the same questions with the same arguments; all that had happened was that they had become more fixed in their opinions and less capable of a becoming modesty in their expression. John drew the quite modern English moral that to linger in abstract dialectic was a waste of time. [1]

We may ask, however, whether the history of philosophy turns out on closer inspection to be quite such a shambles as is often supposed. Is it possible, after all, to discern a central philosophical tradition which persists and develops? Can we talk of a perennial philosophy and, if so, in what sense?

The first question to ask is about the extent to which

[1] John of Salisbury, *Metalogicon*, ii, 10.

151

agreement might be expected in philosophy. It may not be wrong to expect individual personality to count for more in philosophy than in the sciences of external observation. Yet philosophy must aim in its own way at being objective and scientific. Contradictory propositions can no more be simultaneously true in philosophy than in the sciences.

The sciences of external observation and experiment depend on facts which, under suitable conditions and, if necessary, with suitable apparatus, are easily accessible to any number of people. The philosopher may be said to conduct experiments in thinking. In probing the foundations of experience and knowledge he is attempting to make new differentiations of attention and to reach new conceptual discriminations. These are not easy to describe intelligibly; we all know that it often takes a considerable time to begin to grasp the point of a philosophical argument and that is not necessarily due either to our own stupidity or to avoidable obscurity on the part of the philosopher himself. To learn to repeat accurately another philosopher's intellectual gymnastics is a difficult task; again, we know how often students, and even historians of some reputation, can be entirely off the mark in interpreting philosophies with whose terminology they have a nodding acquaintance but whose thought they have obviously been unable to follow.

Consequently, much more of an individual turn of mind is required both for doing philosophy and for learning how other philosophers have done it. Nearly everyone can be taught some elementary physics, but it does not seem possible to teach everyone even what philosophy is about. For some it will continue to be a horror of monstrous words. And everyone has to do his own philosophizing in accordance with his own mental equipment and way of thinking.

While, then, truth will not contradict truth, we cannot expect from philosophers the same measure of uniformity that we expect from scientists at a given stage of the development of a science. In so far as philosophers attain valid results, their results will be mutually complementary, but they may not be easy to fit together. We should expect, therefore, that a deeper understanding of what philosophers have said, although it will not abolish real contradictions, will reconcile some apparent contradictions and will make philosophy seem less of a battlefield where each man is fighting for himself against all the rest. A certain unity or harmony of philosophical experience ought to reveal itself.

That is why a comprehensive knowledge of the history of philosophy is essential to a philosopher. Only familiarity with the great philosophers can show the legitimate variations in the art of philosophizing and can enable a later thinker to pursue his researches on an adequate front and with adequate means. An arbitrary eclecticism is to be condemned for making no sufficient critical effort to discriminate the true from the false, but nowhere more than in philosophy is it desirable to try to grasp the other man's point of view and to see what can really be seen from it.

On another side these reflections show the danger of mere repetitive jargon in philosophy. When the recital of accepted verbal formulas takes the place of an attempt at personal understanding, we have reached the extreme of Byzantinism. For it is not altogether unjust to say that the Eastern Empire preserved the works and the terminology of the Greek thinkers for many centuries without any real attempt to keep the thought alive or to contribute to its development. Byzantinism describes a verbal uniformity which masks an absence of thought.

In spite of all this some forms of linguistic expression are happier than others and rightly tend to be perpetuated. And if we are justified in looking for more harmony among genuine philosophers than appears on the surface, it should be possible to find appropriate language in which to exhibit what they really meant without the appearance of contradiction. Hence, while making due allowance for the personal factor and avoiding mere verbalism, we should expect not only new developments and new ways of thinking in philosophy but a complementary tendency to bring together what is of most value and to merge it in a broad stream of continuing tradition. Such a stream of tradition, carrying down the acquisitions of the past and receiving new tributaries in the present, is what a perennial philosophy ought to be. Can any such central tradition of philosophy be discerned in history?

II

In later Greek philosophy the various systems, Platonic and Aristotelian, Stoic and Epicurean, became more complexly interrelated and showed a tendency to merge. Perhaps this was a more fruitful merging than historians of Greek thought have often supposed. The fact that so much Hellenistic philosophy has perished makes this difficult to judge, but recent historians seem inclined to attribute to it a greater importance than their predecessors did. Certainly Plotinus was a great philosopher, and, although the predominant element in his thought classifies him as a Platonist, he derived much from other sources without meriting the reproach of inconsistency or of being an arbitrary eclectic.

The medieval philosophers, while not expecting all philosophers to agree and without failing to differ considerably among themselves, thought of themselves as recovering not only the conflicting systems of individual philosophers but a great philosophical tradition. That they identified this with Aristotelianism is partly due to the fact that Aristotle was the one Greek philosopher with whose works they had any thorough acquaintance, but, without going to Picavet's extreme and regarding medieval scholasticism as the reestablishment of neoplatonic conclusions on Aristotelian foundations, we can readily admit that Latin Aristotelianism, like its Arabic counterpart, borrowed a great deal from Plato. The "Plato" who served as an occasional whipping-boy for the scholastics is a derivative figure who has little to do with the disciple of Socrates and master of Aristotle.

Yet it is not altogether an historical accident that the medieval philosophical tradition thought of itself as Aristotelian. For Aristotle is above all the systematic philosopher of antiquity. No one did more than Aristotle to determine an appropriate vocabulary for philosophy. Contemporary European thinkers may not be willing Aristotelians, they may not even be conscious Aristotelians, but they can scarcely escape the influence of the thinker who, in creating a philosophical language, gave a permanent direction to European philosophical thought. It is not unreasonable to suggest that the best historical means of formulating a central tradition of philosophy consists in relating the thought of philosophers as closely as possible to the clear and appropriate terminology of Aristotle. This is what the medieval scholastics, as far as their knowledge and opportunity went, tried to do.

If, then, we look at the history of philosophy from antiquity to the Middle Ages, it is no paradox to think of a perennial philosophy in process of formation and development. The contrary impression is due to the violent oppositions in philosophy during the last three centuries. The achievements of philosophy since Descartes are equally obvious. The distinction between philosophy and the sciences of observation has become much clearer, and the primary function of philosophy in criticizing the presuppositions of experience and knowledge is recognized. Fundamental questions have been asked which were scarcely touched upon in antiquity and the Middle Ages.

We must ask ourselves whether the present philosophical anarchy is an inevitable consequence of the kind of question that philosophers now ask. If so, some measure of scepticism follows. If not, we have still to ask whether it is possible to link up again with the philosophical tradition of antiquity and the Middle Ages. Alternatively, if the foundations of the older tradition are irremediably ruined, it may be that we can eventually arrive at greater unanimity, but this will be the beginning of a new tradition.

III

Meanwhile, during approximately the last hundred years, the old tradition has begun to reassert itself. As neo-Scholasticism or neo-Thomism it claims to represent the Latin Aristotelianism of the Middle Ages and to take a place among the movements of contemporary philosophy. It has not, however, achieved more than a modest degree of recognition, and there have recently been signs that some of its original enthusiasm has waned.

A first difficulty is that neo-Thomism may seem to have an unduly large theological axe to grind and to be little more than a sophisticated religious apologetic. Medieval philosophy grew up in organic connection with theology, and the connection of neo-Thomism with Catholic theology is correspondingly close. The solution of this difficulty is not assisted by those conscientious writers of textbooks whose lack of live understanding and failure to take any philosophical problem really seriously is insufficiently compensated by their zeal to follow fashion and to offer a justification of their religious convictions in a passable imitation of the language of St. Thomas.

For a Christian and a Catholic, of course, it is no disadvantage that a philosophical system should harmonize easily with Catholic theology in its traditional form. Yet this circumstance would by itself be a highly unphilosophical reason for adopting a philosophical system. We have no right to suppose that speculative theology should be easy, and sundry attempts to make it easier have been rejected in the past as heresies. Faith belongs to a different dimension of thinking from philosophy, and no systematic philosophy can be imposed in the name of faith. A contemporary Christian is no less a Christian if he feels himself compelled by his own reflection, even if mistakenly, to regard the medieval philosophical framework of theology as outworn.

The real criterion of the value of neo-Thomism as a philosophy is a philosophical one. Is the appropriate answer to the problems of modern and contemporary philosophy one which leads to the recovery of the main positions of that medieval Aristotelianism whose leading representative was St. Thomas Aquinas? If so, we can say that there is still a perennial philosophy.

Here again, unfavourable factors are to be noticed. Too many neo-Thomist writers have been as carefully insulated from contemporary philosophical discussion as other contemporary philosophers are from the appeal of neo-Thomism. If it were possible to revive a medieval system only by adopting the policy of the ostrich towards all that militates against it, the dispassionate observer would be justified in feeling suspicion.

In spite of all unfavourable factors, however, this book is offered as some contribution towards bridging the gap. For, when all the difficulties have been taken into account, the gap can and should be bridged. Reflection on modern philosophy suggests that an unduly restricted view has been taken both of the contents of experience and of the power of thought. It was right to criticize the foundations of knowledge as thoroughly as possible, but men have lingered too long in hesitant or negative answers to their problems. A critical scrutiny of foundations which is not merely negative does not entail the demolition of the older metaphysical philosophy, whether that demolition be regarded as permanent or as a prelude to the erection of something different.

The older philosophy must itself, of course, be rethought in relation to later problems and later needs. But it has not only to be brought into relation with modern ideas; it also requires to continue to draw life from its original sources. The Greeks, and especially Plato and Aristotle, remain the fountainheads of European philosophy. If the defects of some modern philosophers are due to not bothering about anything earlier than Descartes, the defects of some neo-Thomists are due to stopping short at the Middle Ages and failing to go back sufficiently to the Greek sources of their philosophical tradition.

If, then, we are asked whether there is a perennial philosophy, our answer is that in principle there is such a philosophy, leading from Plato and Aristotle to the Middle Ages and waiting to be supplemented by the positive results of more recent thought. In practice the re-establishment of such a philosophy is a work in process, and we have tried to indicate some of the conditions for its successful outcome. Above all, the different schools of philosophy need to learn to understand one another and to be able to enter into fruitful debate. It is as a contribution to work in process, and not as a description of work accomplished, that this essay is designed.